Praise for Nathan Aguinaga's Previous Work

LIFER

"*Lifer* is an insightful behind-the-curtain look into the life and career of a US Army Infantry paratrooper and a must read for other combat veterans regardless of service."

—**COLONEL CARL D. MATTER**, US Marine Corps (Retired)

ONE TERM

"A powerful book about today's divide among our country and the personal divide that exists within our families as well."

—**SENIOR CHIEF PETTY OFFICER THOMAS LEE**, US Navy (Retired)

WAKE UP, YOU'RE HAVING ANOTHER NIGHTMARE

"An extremely remarkable book created with fearlessness, strength, honesty and every other ingredient that phenomenal soldiers are made of."

—**COLONEL JOHN SCHWEMMER**, US Army

Finding My Son: A Story of a Family Finding Each Other

by Nathan Aguinaga

© Copyright 2025 Nathan Aguinaga

ISBN 979-8-88824-587-3

All rights reserved. No part of this publication may be reproduced, stored in a retrieval system, or transmitted in any form or by any means—electronic, mechanical, photocopy, recording, or any other—except for brief quotations in printed reviews, without the prior written permission of the author.

Published by

◀ köehlerbooks™

3705 Shore Drive
Virginia Beach, VA 23455
800-435-4811
www.koehlerbooks.com

FINDING MY SON

FINDING MY SON

A Story of a Family
Finding Each Other

NATHAN AGUINAGA

VIRGINIA BEACH
CAPE CHARLES

CONTENTS

INTRODUCTION ix

CHAPTER 1 1

CHAPTER 2 7

CHAPTER 3 17

CHAPTER 4 27

CHAPTER 5 49

CHAPTER 6 59

CHAPTER 7 67

ACKNOWLEDGMENTS 79

INTRODUCTION

Make no mistake about it. These are actual events that happened in my life and realities that I found out about just a short time ago. I have a twenty-seven-year-old son and two beautiful grandchildren. It's not every Christmas season that you find out that you have an entire family you didn't know you had living approximately 725 miles away.

My newly discovered son Trey recently found my daughter Madyson on 23andMe and had contacted her through the website. This happened maybe a day or two after Christmas of 2023. She had called me to tell me the news of what I expected throughout the past couple of decades: that I had a son in North Carolina somewhere. Not only do I have a son, but I also discovered I have two young grandchildren as well. A four-year-old grandson named Jackson, and a two-year-old granddaughter named Isabelle.

When my wife and I found out about our new family, we were ecstatic and were filled with instant joy. More so for me, I felt a powerful relief of what I had expected and knew in the back of my mind and heart after all of these years—that I had a son living in North Carolina.

As I write this story, Trey, his girlfriend Shannon, my wife Jessica, my daughter Madyson, and my son Taylor have been in constant contact with each other. Now that the shock and awe of all of this is over, we're now at the stage of calling each other and having general conversations. How was your day? How was work? How's the family doing? Et cetera.

In the following chapters, I will explain how all of this came to be throughout the last three decades. I am so excited to be writing this story that is truly a miracle that I believe was meant to be.

CHAPTER 1

North Carolina, Spring of 1995

I was a young soldier who had just turned twenty-three. It was my first spring while serving at Fort Bragg, North Carolina. It was a great time in my life. I was finally serving in the 82nd Airborne Division, which I had reenlisted for during my recent tour in Germany. All of my new friends were from small towns throughout the country, and we had everything in common. We were all single, living in the barracks. We worked hard and played hard. It was nothing to hear loud music blaring down the hallways of the barracks. Everyone kept their doors open and would go from room to room drinking beer and doing shots of whiskey. Rage Against the Machine, Sound Garden, and Tool would be blaring and echoing throughout the hallways. I'm not talking about Friday or Saturday nights either. This was every night during the week. Around 9:00 or 10:00 p.m., it was time to leave the party in the barracks and head to the clubs in Fayetteville, the city that surrounds Fort Bragg. We would dance and party at the clubs like it was our job. We actually considered it our secondary job. Sometimes, when you're young, partying feels like your primary occupation; being in the Army was simply a means to a paycheck that allowed us to have the lifestyle. I discuss this lifestyle in more detail in my previous books, *Division* and *Lifer*, which are based on my time in the 82nd Airborne Division.

At the time, I lived on the second floor of the barracks. My best friend Matt lived on the first floor. I spent most of my time in the barracks down in his room. I'm not going to lie—this was primarily because he always had good looking girls hanging out with him. He was a chick magnet that girls would cling to every weekend. There was one girl I noticed him spending more and more time with on a regular basis. Her name was Bridget. She was a nice girl from Raleigh, which is about fifty miles away from Fort Bragg. It was nothing to see girls in the barracks from cities that were a little farther away, because we would all travel to some of the clubs in Raleigh, Greensboro, and, on occasion, party at University of North Carolina, Chapel Hill.

One weekend morning, I walked downstairs to Matt's room with a cup of coffee, and Bridget was in there.

"Hey, good morning, you two," I said to them.

Bridget looked at me and asked, "Hey, Nate, how come I never see you with a girl here in the barracks?"

"Because I always kick them out before the sun comes up, I guess," I replied sarcastically, smiling at her as I sipped my coffee. They both laughed. "I don't know. I guess I haven't found a girl that I want to date," I added.

At this time, I had only been at Fort Bragg less than six months.

"Well, I have a friend that I work with from Durham that I could introduce to you. She's a very pretty girl who is just getting out of a relationship. Would you like to meet her?"

I asked all the questions of a young man: How old is she? What does she look like? Is she nice? Is she mean? Et cetera. She told me that she was twenty years old and gorgeous.

"Yeah, when can I meet her?" I asked.

"Well, what are you guys doing today?" she asked.

"Just hanging out—it's Sunday; nothing planned with me."

Bridget made a couple phone calls on my buddy's landline phone. This was long before cell phones. As a matter of fact, she had asked him permission to make long-distance calls because back in those days, you had to pay for them on your monthly phone bill. I even told him that I would pay for them when he got his next bill because Bridget was trying to hook me up with this girl.

Now this girl lived in Durham, but this weekend, she was staying with her older sister in Greensboro. Bridget had told me her name was Crystal and that she was twenty years old.

After Bridget found out where she was, we all got cleaned up and dressed and headed off to Greensboro. From Fort Bragg, Greensboro was closer than driving to Durham, straight north about fifty miles. Her sister and brother-in-law had a house up there in town.

When I first met Crystal, I couldn't believe how beautiful she was. She was gorgeous. She was petite with dark, straight hair and piercing blue eyes. I was immediately nervous once I saw her. I said hello to her as Bridget introduced me and my buddy to her. I was also introduced to her sister, who was very polite. Crystal said hello back to me as I stood there melting over her beauty and her sweet little southern accent.

We talked and visited for a while. I told her about where I was from in Michigan and all about joining and serving in the Army. She did the same with me, telling me all about her family in Durham. We made small talk for about an hour or so, until she told me she had three kids. Her kids were not with her that weekend; they were staying at her mom and dad's back in Durham. At the time, her oldest was around four, the second child was around two, and her youngest was just a baby—around eight or nine months old.

For many young soldiers in their early twenties, a girl telling them that she had children might deter them from wanting to date her. But for me, after seeing this girl's beauty and her positive, kind personality, it didn't matter at all.

We eventually all went out to lunch and had a great afternoon together. When we were done, she needed to get back to her parents' house and pick up her kids. She rode back with Bridget, and Matt and I were in his truck going the opposite direction back to Bragg. While at the restaurant, we exchanged phone numbers, which I had been nervous to ask her to do. She didn't even hesitate, which told me that perhaps she was interested in me too. When we parted from one another in the parking lot, we shook hands and even gave each other a little "tap-tap hug."

"Do you mind if I call you tonight?" I asked her.

"Absolutely, I'm looking forward to it," she sweetly replied.

I knew of "love at first sight," but that day, I began to think that the concept was true.

On the highway back to Fort Bragg, I looked at Matt and asked him what he thought about her. He didn't hesitate to tell me that he thought she was gorgeous. Actually, he said that she was "pretty hot." I was on cloud nine all the way back to base, which was about an hour and some change from Greensboro. That evening, I called Crystal, and her and I talked for about an hour. For the remainder of the week, we talked every night and started to get to know each other.

We had all made plans to go to Bridget's house in Raleigh the next weekend. Bridget was staying with and renting a room from a friend of hers. I believe she was older, and the two of them were coworkers. It was a nice little brick house within a little suburb away from the city. It was a typical Friday night of two couples in their early twenties. Socializing, listening to music, drinking beer and wine and an occasional shot or two of whiskey.

After playing some drinking games in Bridget's kitchen until well after 1:00 a.m., it was time to go to sleep. I was nervous and said that I would sleep on the couch or the floor in the living room. Bridget's house only had two bedrooms. Her roommate was out of town for the weekend, so Bridget and Matt took her bedroom. She told Crystal that she could stay in her room. Crystal looked at me and said that it was nonsense for me to sleep on the couch or on the floor; I could sleep with her. Are you kidding me? I didn't hesitate to take her up on her offer.

"Are you sure?" I asked her.

"C'mon," she said as she grabbed my hand, and we walked into Bridget's room together.

That night was the first time Crystal and I were together, and at that point, I had fallen in love with her. Again, another phrase—"making love"—became a reality for me that night.

CHAPTER 2

My First Girlfriend

It was about a two-hour drive one way to get to Crystal's house in Durham from my barracks at Fort Bragg. She lived in a little white house on a hill. The back of the house overlooked a valley. Her parents lived a couple of miles down the road in a little suburban neighborhood. They were good people who accepted me immediately. Her mom and stepdad owned a large camper that they kept parked in their driveway. From time to time, Crystal and I would stay in it when we would go visit them on weekends. They were cool parents, genuine, easygoing people. They liked to drink beer, play cards, and have a good time. Not only did I fall in love with Crystal, but I also had a strong admiration for her parents. It was like having a family away from my family—who were all back in Michigan—while I served in the Army in North Carolina.

As I mentioned earlier, Crystal and her boyfriend had recently broken up. He was the father of her three children. When I was going to meet him for the first time, I was nervous. This wasn't just an ordinary ex-boyfriend, but the daddy of her babies. So, I had anxiety the first time he dropped off the kids and I was sitting in Crystal's living room. He walked through the door with the kids, looked down at me as I was sitting on the couch, and stuck out his hand for a handshake. I stood up, shook his hand, and introduced myself to him.

"I'm Steve," he said to me.

"It's nice to meet you, Steve. I'm Nate."

"So, you're in the Army at Fort Bragg?" he asked.

"Yeah, I've been there for about six months."

"Well, thanks for your service."

I was immediately impressed with his demeanor toward me and felt at ease. I had assumed that the first contact we would have with each other would be awkward, or even somewhat hostile, but it wasn't at all.

I was now not only in love with this young lady, but I was comfortable around her entire family. It was the most at peace that I had felt in a long time. I loved being a paratrooper at Fort Bragg, and my career in the Army as a whole, and now, I loved being with this young, beautiful girl. It was a great time in my life. About a year earlier, I had divorced my ex-wife, who was my high school sweetheart. We were married for less than two years by the time we separated, when I was at my previous duty station in Germany. Crystal was my first relationship since my divorce. The only strange part about me getting into this relationship was that my ex-wife had the same name, except she spelled it with a K. One could argue that another strange part about me dating Crystal was that she had three small children, but it didn't faze me at all. At this point in my life, my priority was my happiness.

Crystal and Steve would alternate weekends with their children. When he had the kids, she would spend the weekends with me at Fort Bragg. She stayed right in my barracks room with me. I had my own room, anyway, so there weren't other soldiers staying with us. Don't get me wrong, there were soldiers who didn't care. They would bring girls back to the barracks and wouldn't care if there were roommates or not. The barracks were kind of like a university dorm, maybe even a little bit wilder. Never had I stayed in a college dorm, but I would almost bet that the 82nd Airborne Division barracks were a lot wilder, especially on weekends. Since we were in an all-male barracks, I would escort her to our public restroom, or the latrine, as we referred to it. I would stand outside the door and not allow any other soldiers to enter until she was done. She even showered in it as well, since she usually spent the entire weekends there with me. Her staying with me for an entire weekend in the barracks would never fly today. This was before 9/11, and the standards of civilians on military installations were laid back. Even in the mid-'90s, we were not allowed to have females in the barracks past midnight. It was so easy back then for us to have girls the whole weekend with us, and the sergeants in the barracks never said a word. All of us had girlfriends that stayed the weekends. It was a common thing.

She got along with all my friends in my unit. We would all party, drink beer, and listen to hard rock. All the room doors were open, and everyone had a booming stereo system. That was the thing when you were a young single soldier. You usually bought yourself your first vehicle and a heavy stereo system to rock out with every night. Nobody ever told you to turn it down either. It was literally a twenty-four-seven party.

When it was Crystal's weekend to have the kids, I would stay at her house with her in Durham. We would hang out, watch movies, go to the mall, and visit her parents. They were relaxing weekends. Her kids were good too. They were respectful, mostly quiet, and well-behaved. When I would get a long weekend from the Army, I would spend it at her house. We would have a four-day weekend, so I would leave the barracks after work on a Thursday and stay with Crystal and her family until Monday evening. Sometimes, I would stay with her until Tuesday morning, get up at 3:00 a.m., and drive two hours back to Bragg. I did that a few times during our time together. One morning when Crystal was at work, her dad came over for coffee, and he and I were watching the news. It was breaking news of the Oklahoma City bombing that had just taken place that morning. It was the first time anyone had ever heard the name of Timothy McVeigh. Her dad and I sat there in disbelief while the story broke. We couldn't believe this could happen in the United States. It was the most tragic moment of terrorism in my lifetime, until about six, almost seven years later.

When I would watch the kids while she was at work on a Friday or Monday, depending how long our weekend was from my unit at Fort Bragg, we would spend the days watching cartoons. Mainly *Looney Tunes*. To this day, I could sit and watch Bugs Bunny and *Looney Tunes* for hours, laughing myself to death. The youngest child was just a baby. She was adorable and had a little personality even at age ten or eleven months old. I was nervous being with a baby, but it all came back to me from when I was a teenager taking care of my little brother when he was a baby. Her parents would stop in throughout the day to see if I needed help and make sure everything was all right.

Around two months into my relationship with Crystal, Matt came up to my room in the barracks one day after work and asked if I wanted to go shopping with him at the Fayetteville mall. We were in our early twenties and had our first vehicles, great stereo systems in our rooms, and nice clothes. Back in those days it was Guess jeans, Timberlands or Doc Martens, and Tommy Hilfiger shirts, maybe even Nautica.

As we walked through the mall, we passed by one of the several jewelry stores.

"Hey, dude," I said to Matt. "Let's walk in here; I want to check out some rings."

"Rings, for what?" Matt asked, confused.

"I just want to check them out, that's all. I'm just curious."

"You want to buy a ring for your girlfriend in Durham, don't you?"

"Maybe something small and not too expensive."

I asked for a ring that had the smallest diamond on it. I can't remember how much it was exactly, but it was probably around $120—which was a lot for an Army E-4 specialist in 1995. Matt told me I was lucky that she was so pretty and sweet, or he would have given me a hard time for buying a girl a ring that I had only been dating for two months. I told him that for the first time since I'd been in the Army, I had met a girl that I could trust. She was a homebody who took care of her kids. If she wasn't at home, she was at her parents or with me. Prior to her, I'd had other girls that I had been with, and they were fun, but they were mostly clubgoers throughout Fayetteville, Raleigh, or Greensboro.

There were even times when I would feel somewhat bad for Crystal, because she was so young and already playing the mother role with three small children instead of being an average twenty-year-old going out with friends. However, she was content with her lifestyle, and the reality was that she was getting away at times with me back at Fort Bragg or all of us hanging out at Bridget's house in Raleigh.

I showed up to her house on a Friday evening after I got out of work. I had the ring in my overnight bag and couldn't wait to surprise her with it. I didn't consider it an engagement ring, but more of a "let's be steady" promise ring. I didn't pull it out of my bag right away, but wanted to ease into it a little later, after we had a few drinks. She was being quiet with me throughout the evening. She was tending more to her kids, and I was more or less sitting there watching the television. Her conversations with me were short. I had a feeling that something was wrong or that something had happened. All kinds of thoughts were going through my mind.

Either way, I still got up and walked over to her bedroom where I had set my bag down. I grabbed it and pulled out the ring. I went over to the couch and sat down next to her. She was holding the baby and continued to be silent. I handed her the box.

"Here you go, sweetheart, this is for you."

"What is this, Nate?" she asked. It was obvious what it was.

"It's just a little something I picked up from the mall this week for you."

She opened the box and stared at the ring. She then closed it and turned her head toward me.

"I cannot accept this from you, Nate," she said softly.

I looked at her, confused, and asked her why not. I even conveyed to her that it wasn't an engagement ring, but more of a promise ring.

"Not only can I not accept this, but I don't think we should see each other anymore," she said.

"Are you serious?" I had no idea that this was going to happen this weekend when I left Bragg for Durham. I was in a state of shock. She handed me the box back.

"I had a long talk with my parents and Steve this week, and we all believe that it would be in all of our best interests that we split up. It would be the Christian thing to do, especially since Steve and I have three children together. You're such a nice guy and very caring, and we had a great time together these past couple of months, but I need to do the right thing and have the kids back with their father." My heart immediately sank as I sat there silently. "I'm sorry, Nate," she said to me.

"Yeah, me too, Crystal."

I got up, put the ring back in my bag, and stood there in disbelief for a few seconds.

"Are you sure about this, Crystal?"

"Yes, I am. It's what needs to happen, Nate." I just stood there and shook my head, still in disbelief.

"Okay Crystal, good luck, and have a great life."

I grabbed my bag, and as I was heading toward the door, I looked down and noticed that she was crying on the couch, still holding the baby.

As I drove back toward Fayetteville, I couldn't stop thinking of that image of her as I left. I didn't think she wanted me out of her life. I think she was doing it more for her parents. Perhaps they had been guilting her the entire time that we had been together, and that they finally broke her mentally and emotionally. I tried to make sense of what had just happened that evening, but I couldn't. There was zero arguing between us; we never even had a disagreement. Going to her place and spending time together was like a mini vacation every weekend from the stresses of daily life in the military, especially in the 82nd Airborne Division. Now, it was all over—just like that. It was a long ride home. I didn't even put the radio on.

When I got to the barracks, there was partying going on with plenty of music blaring down the hallways. I went to my room, shut and locked my door, and went to sleep. Well, to be honest, I laid in my bed, staring up at the ceiling. I was still in a state of shock. Did this really happen tonight? I asked myself. I thought about how I had been in such a great mood all day because I knew that after work, I'd be driving to Durham to spend the weekend with my girlfriend. Life changes just like that.

The next morning, I walked downstairs to Matt's room. He was in there with Bridget.

"Nate, what the hell are you doing here? I thought you went to Crystal's this weekend," he asked, confused.

"I did, and now I'm back. I'm not going to beat around the bush; Crystal broke up with me last night, so I drove home."

Bridget looked at me as if she already knew about it.

"What, Bridget? Did you know she was going to break up with me?" I asked desperately. She admitted that Crystal had mentioned it to her at work during the week. I asked her what the real reason was. She repeated the same thing that Crystal had said to me—that it was the right thing to do.

After a couple cups of coffee, we all got ready for the day and went out to breakfast at IHOP. Afterward, we drove over to the mall so that I could return the ring. When I got to the jewelry store, the lady at the counter looked at me like she couldn't understand why I would return it. I felt it wasn't necessary for me to give her details of my personal life events. I told her that I wanted to return it and get my money back. There was a penalty charge of twenty percent. So, for a $120 ring, I got under a hundred bucks back. This was the city of Fayetteville; anything to take money from a soldier. I didn't lose any sleep over it, but the whole situation was frustrating. Actually, I could have done without that entire weekend. Now that I look back on that entire experience at my current age of fifty-two, it was a young adult learning experience that doesn't need to be repeated. In other words, do not fall for somebody so quickly again; no matter how pretty or sweet you think they are.

The next week, we had a field training exercise that would last for about two weeks straight in the Fort Bragg woods. These exercises, for the most part, sucked, and living outside for weeks at a time was uncomfortable. During the day, it was either too hot, or too hot and raining. Then it would be too hot and muggy. At night, if you weren't pulling security on the perimeter or on a combat patrol mission, you slept on the ground under a poncho, fighting off mosquitoes. I remember to this day what kept us going with a positive attitude throughout all the field training days was the thought of going back to the barracks and getting out of the discomfort of the woods and back into the air-conditioning. If you had a girlfriend or a wife to go home to, there was that much more to look forward to getting out of "the field," as we called it.

That first field exercise after Crystal broke up with me was miserable. I was saddened by the fact that I had nobody to go back to when we would return to the garrison and back to the barracks. I eventually had to come to the reality that there was nothing I could do about it, so I had to simply keep going, being as positive as I could be.

About a month went by, and we were deep into the summer of '95. I still thought about Crystal from time to time. I thought about her until I went downstairs one morning to say hi to Matt. When I walked into his room, there was Bridget and two other girls. Both of them were young and beautiful.

"Hello ladies," I said. Who are these cute little things sitting on your couch, my friend?"

They both looked at me with smiles on their faces. I caught them out of the corner of my eye as Bridget introduced them to me. They were both looking at each other as they giggled. They were both cute, but I was impressed more with the brunette girl; the other was more of a dirty blonde. She stuck her hand out to shake mine, but instead, I leaned over and kissed it gently. I thought I was a Rico Suave back in my younger years. Either way, she bought into it and referred to me as a gentleman. Her name was Erin, and she was young and beautiful. I wasn't sure how young, though. I was guessing around nineteen. I knew she was at least eighteen to be able to get into the barracks. Our unit standard was that all visitors had to show ID to the front desk sergeant in order to enter. I didn't care.

"How old are you, young lady? You old enough to be in here?"

She looked at her friend, whose name was Paula, and giggled again.

"I'm eighteen, she answered."

"You still in high school?" I asked jokingly. Again, she giggled.

"No, I graduated a couple of months ago." Yes, she was a young girl, but a legal adult, to say the least.

After an hour of visiting my new friend, Bridget asked if Matt and I would like to go back to Raleigh with them and visit; maybe we could stop and get some lunch on the way. We both agreed. I went back upstairs to shower and get ready, and then the two of us followed all of them in Matt's truck.

"Dude, what do you think of that Erin girl?" I asked Matt.

He answered, "Oh man, she is hot. Do you think you're going to try to hook up with her?"

"I'm going to at least get her phone number and go from there. I remember the last girl that Bridget hooked me up with. Maybe this is just what I need to get my mind off of her." Matt agreed.

That evening, right before we left Raleigh, Erin and I exchanged phone numbers before we said goodbye to each other. Before we got into Matt's truck, I leaned over and kissed her. We probably kissed for about two or three minutes. It was starting to get a little hot and heavy, but it was still innocent. I mean, we were standing outside of the truck, in the open. We talked on the phone all that week. A couple of weeks later, we were officially boyfriend and girlfriend. Crystal was finally out of my mind.

CHAPTER 3

A Reconnection

A full year went by, and now it was the summer of 1996. After six months of dating Erin, we had broken up. We attempted to go back and forth in order to try to see if there was any love left, but it didn't exist. She was too young to want to have a serious relationship with anyone. I was twenty-four, and I was feeling the same way. We both wanted to play the field and have fun. Being in the active-duty military is almost impossible to maintain a solid, strong relationship. Especially when couples are so young. Assignments to a rapid deployment unit, like the 82nd Airborne Division, makes it even that much harder, because you're gone most of the time. We were either deployed for a month to Panama, or Fort Polk, Louisiana, or in a two- or three-week field exercise on Fort Bragg. If you weren't engaged in any of these criteria, you were in a military school. We were always separated from the ones we loved, so permanent relationships were almost non-existent, including marriages.

Bridget and Matt had broken up as well. When I was with Erin, Bridget had started seeing my other friend, Mike. It was a good time, and we all had fun hanging out together that year and a half. However, I had a big change in my life and in my military career. I had made the rank of sergeant, which comes along with obvious leadership responsibilities. So, by this time, I was more focused on getting settled into my new duty position, which was an infantry team leader, in charge of three other soldiers. I had already reenlisted once, therefore, my mind was set on doing this as a career. By this time, I had over five years in the Army, from the age of eighteen.

I remember sitting in my barracks room one night watching a movie with Mike. All of a sudden, my phone rang. Since this was before cell phones, we all had landline phones in our rooms, and our numbers were listed in the Fayetteville phone book. There were no "scams likely" that would show up. If your phone rang in those days, it was probably either somebody who truly wanted to talk to you or a wrong number.

I answered, and it was Bridget from Raleigh.

"Hey, how's it going, Bridget? It's been a while," I said to her.

"Hi Nate. I have someone here that would like to say hello."

"Well, put that person on the phone, I guess."

"Hello, Nathan."

It was a girl with somewhat of a tiny, quiet, but strong southern accent. Of course, it was North Carolina. At first, I couldn't recognize it. In the Carolinas, the accents sounded the same to me.

"Who's this that I have the pleasure of talking to?" I asked.

"It's Crystal."

"Crystal from Durham?" I asked. I was confused about why she would want to say hi and talk to me after an entire year of not communicating or seeing each other. "Well, hi, Crystal, how are you?"

"I'm fine. Never mind me. How have you been, Nathan?"

We exchanged pleasantries. I asked about her kids and her parents. I think I even asked about her boyfriend. She had admitted to me that the two of them had been on and off for the past few months again. At that point, I realized that this relationship with the father of her children was an ongoing on-and-off situation.

It was nice hearing from her again, even after all this time had gone by. We talked for about a good half-hour. Eventually, I had asked her if she would like to get together for dinner the upcoming weekend. She had agreed. I had asked her if she remembered how to get to the barracks. She said she did, but I had to tell her that I was in a different building than before. I was still in the same row of buildings but had moved companies due to my recent promotion. I told her I was in the first building from the parking lot that she remembered from a year ago. She assured me that she would find me.

Early that Friday evening, the company Charge of Quarters (CQ) sent his runner up to my room to tell me that there was a girl downstairs to see me. I went down to the CQ desk, and there she was, looking as beautiful as she did a year ago.

"Hey, how are you? It's great to see you again!" I said to her as I gave her a quick little hug.

"I'm fine. It's great to see you again, Nate," she said.

"Well, would you like to go to dinner?" I asked.

"Sure, that would be nice."

"Okay, let's go. I'm already if you are."

We walked out of the company and to the parking lot. She noticed I still had the same little red truck that I had when we dated a year ago.

"Yep, that's the same vehicle. I just paid it off a couple of weeks ago."

It was my way of easing up the atmosphere a little bit. We were both nervous to see each other, especially with the way that we parted last time we had seen each other.

I took her to a bar and grill in Fayetteville. I believe it was Bennigan's, which today is out of business. Why they closed permanently, I have no idea. Back in the '90s, it was the hot spot to go to, at least in the south. It was always packed too. My buddies and I used to go there at least twice a week.

While Crystal and I were having a beer, waiting on our dinner, I finally reached for the courage to ask her how she and her boyfriend were doing. I already knew the answer. If she were willing to travel two hours away from Durham to spend the evening with me, that probably meant they weren't doing too well in their relationship. She told me exactly that. Their relationship had been on the rocks for the past couple of months, and she felt it was time for her to get away for an evening. That's where I came in. I asked her if she had had another relationship with someone else in between me and the two of them getting back together. She said she didn't, and I believed her. Why else would she drive two hours to spend an evening with me?

We had a great time together. We must have stayed at the restaurant for at least three hours total. The atmosphere was relaxing and had lightened up from when she first arrived at my barracks. I'm sure the alcohol we were steadily drinking helped as well. She told me all about her kids and how big they were getting as I told her about my days at Fort Bragg over the past year. I finally got the guts to ask her what she wanted to do for the rest of the night.

"Would you like to go out? Maybe to a movie, or a nightclub, or something?" I asked.

"No," she replied. "I'd rather spend the night alone with you, if you're okay with that?"

I wasn't going to turn that opportunity down. She practically read my mind. Actually, she read my mind completely.

It only took me a few seconds to come up with the idea of getting a nice hotel for the evening. I wasn't going to offer for her to stay in my barracks room with me like we used to do before. Instead, we would stay at a nearby Holiday Inn Express. Plus, I wouldn't have to drive that far, especially back onto the military installation after I'd been drinking. That is an easy way to get a DUI, trying to drive through the main gate of Fort Bragg. All the military police have to do is smell alcohol in the vehicle and they would tell you to park it, get out, and start a sobriety test. If the servicemember fails, they would automatically be arrested, and taken to the MP station until a senior ranking individual came to sign you out. Once back at your unit, the soldier would face an automatic field-grade punishment. This was a reduction in rank, forfeiture of up to two months' pay, and restriction to the barracks for a certain number of weeks. Alcohol or drug-related incidences were common throughout the Army.

Before going to the Holiday Inn, I stopped at the closest liquor store and got us some alcohol to take back with us. Once in our room, I poured us a drink, and we toasted to us having a romantic evening together. I don't think we finished that drink before we were all over each other. I won't get into details, but I think you can figure the rest out. Let's just say that it was a long, romantic evening. I don't think we even turned on the television.

The next morning, I got up and went downstairs to the lobby. I needed a toothbrush and some toothpaste. After we both brushed our teeth, we took a shower together. It was nice; almost like something out of a movie. I checked us out of the hotel then we walked over to the IHOP, which was in the same parking lot. I asked her during breakfast if she wanted to stay another night, but she said she had to get back to her kids in Durham. She told me that her intention was to just get away for a night.

"I had a great night with you, Nate. It was so refreshing to see you again. I am sorry about the way things ended up before, but at the time, I felt it was the right thing to do."

As I took a sip of my coffee, I nodded in agreement.

"Yeah, it was, Crystal," I said. Where do we go from here? Or do we go anywhere?"

"I think we should just take it slow and stay as friends for now," she said, almost sadly.

At that point, it hit me like a lightning bolt. That was almost music to my ears, because deep down, I was sure that the trust factor was never going to be there with this girl again. When I had talked to her on the phone earlier that week, I was so excited that I was going to see her again—and I was, make no mistake about it.

However, being with her this time, I had told myself this was a weekend thing, a one-night stand for old times' sake. Again, the trust factor wasn't there anymore. I kept telling myself that no matter what, the father of her children would forever be in her life. If I did go back to being serious with her, how long would it take before she would break up with me and go back to Steve again? It was like the old saying: "Screw me once, shame on you. Screw me twice, shame on me."

After breakfast, we drove back to the barracks parking lot. I dropped her off at her car, got out of my truck, and gave her a hug and a kiss.

"Thank you for contacting me again, Crystal. I had an awesome evening with you. I needed that night out. You are a beautiful girl. Get a hold of me; you have my number. Like you said, let's be friends. But I hope you don't stay away for another year this time."

She laughed. "I won't. I had an awesome night with you, Nate. Thank you for such a great night that I very much needed. I will call you soon. I'd like to see you again soon," she said.

"Sure thing," I said. "I'll be looking forward to your call. If I don't answer, it's because I'm not in my room. Just leave a message on my machine and I'll call you back, okay?"

We gave each other another hug and a kiss on the lips, and I told her to drive safely back home.

When I got back up to my barracks room, I turned on my Metallica *Ride the Lightning* CD and reached for the refrigerator door, pulled out a Miller Lite bottle of beer, lit up a Marlboro Red cigarette, and the party began. It was after noon. So, I opened my door and let the music flow down the hallway. The next thing you know, dudes started entering my room. A couple of them had girls with them who had spent the night. We partied all day and well into the night. It was a glorious time of our youth.

A couple of weeks went by, and it was your usual Saturday in the barracks. Yes, we were partying again. I was out in the hallway talking to some girl I didn't know, but apparently, she had been there with some other soldier from the previous night. Some dude came out of my room and said there was some girl on the phone for me.

"Hello, this is Nate."

"Hi there, this is Crystal. How are you doing?"

"Oh, hey! I'm fine, how are you? What are you up to today?"

"Well, I spent the night at Bridget's last night, and we were wondering if you wouldn't mind if we come down your way today?"

"Hell yes! C'mon down here," I said. "Actually, we're just doing the norm and partying in the barracks. You and Bridget c'mon down like the old days. It'll be fun."

"Okay, Nate! We'll be down there in about an hour and some change."

"Okay. Oh, yeah, what do you guys want to drink? I'll make sure I have it here for you by the time you get here."

"Oh, we'll bring our leftovers from last night. We'll pack it in a cooler. You don't have to buy us anything."

After I hung up, I drank one more beer, got some clean clothes and went to the latrine to take a shower. I didn't even kick anyone out of my room.

Unfortunately, that Saturday, our battalion had an ass for a staff duty sergeant. This guy was a stickler for the rules. He kept coming over to our party in the barracks, telling us we needed to turn down the music and to quiet it down. He came over three or four times throughout the day and night. He even warned us guys that he was going to inspect the barracks after 10:00, or 2200 hours, in order to ensure that all the females were out. He had our company CQ with him and was even threatening him that if he didn't enforce the rules in our company barracks, he was going to turn him in to the chain of command. This dude was a real tool bag. Of all nights we had to get an ass for a staff duty NCO, it had to be the night I had Crystal with me.

I was debating whether or not to drive on post to get a room at the lodge in order to avoid the hassle of this guy and prevent myself from getting into trouble Monday morning. The only problem was that we had all been drinking all day and into the evening. I didn't want to risk drinking and driving on base. "What do I do, what do I do?" I kept asking myself. There was no way that I was going to make Crystal and Bridget leave Fort Bragg and drive all the way back to Raleigh at 10:00 at night.

It was about 9:30 when I came up with a plan. Bridget was interested in a guy who lived next door to me. I got with him and told him that I had a plan to keep the girls overnight without getting busted by the staff duty guy. My plan was this: we would walk the girls out at ten, right past the CQ's desk. I would bet anything that the battalion staff duty NCO (Mr. Jack-ass) would be standing there to ensure that all females left the barracks on time. He knew that we were partying and had physically seen all the girls in our barracks. Therefore, he would be damned if he would have missed the opportunity to catch us keeping some of them in our rooms. Unfortunately for him, we were smarter than he was. Once we would say goodbye to the ladies in front of the staff duty, we would head back upstairs and have the girls climb up the fire escape ladder to the second-floor roof, which was located in the rear of the building. From there, we would let them in through the window of my barracks room. I figured that was our best way to get away with staying with the girls.

I talked to Crystal and Bridget about it and asked them what they thought about this attempt; if they were willing to take the chance. They both agreed and were even excited about attempting it. I'll admit, just the idea of it was kind of fun and exciting. Worst case scenario, we could have paid for a cab and had the driver drop us off at the base lodge for the night, but we were a little short on cash since it was the end of the month. It would have been "ghetto" to ask the girls to pay for us, so we stuck to our deviant plan of getting them both back into the barracks.

We walked them downstairs to the CQ desk, which was right at the main entrance of the barracks. There were other entrances, but at night, they were locked and chained for security purposes. The only way in or out of the barracks was through the doors at the CQ. Lo and behold, there he was, standing next to the doors, just like I predicted—the staff duty guy. I figured I'd put on a little show and exaggerate the situation a little bit for him. I gave Crystal a hug and a kiss and told her goodbye and that I would see her in the morning. I extended the goodbye for about a good thirty seconds, in order to ensure that he witnessed it. When the two of us were convinced that he saw the girls walk out and leave the barracks, we turned around and walked past the desk. My colleague even said, "Man, I wish they could have stayed like the old days."

The staff duty looked at us and said, "Well, guys, I'm sorry, but rules are rules. soldiers. Make sure you keep the music down for the rest of the night. It's well after 2200 now."

"Yes, Sergeant, will do," we both said simultaneously.

As we turned the corner and headed toward the stairwell and back up to the second floor, I could hear him telling the CQ goodnight and to let him know if there's any trouble during the remainder of the night. I looked at my buddy as we were walking up the stairs and smiled at him.

When we got back to my room, I opened my window and looked out for the girls. They showed up on the roof and crawled through my window. Bridget went next door with my buddy, while Crystal and I stayed in my room. I had already turned off the lights in the hallway to conceal Bridget as she walked out of my room. I turned on the television, got us a couple of beers, and we sat on my couch and talked. Again, Crystal and I had a nice, romantic evening. We didn't fall asleep until almost 5:00 a.m.

By the time we woke up, it was almost noon. We both walked down to the latrine to go to the bathroom and brush our teeth. I didn't have to worry about her being seen this time. We were authorized to have women in the barracks by this time of the day, plus, the staff duty and CQ had already changed over by 9:00 that morning, anyway.

We asked the girls if they wanted to go to breakfast with us. They agreed, but they needed to leave from there to head straight back to Raleigh and Durham afterward. Crystal had to pick up her kids from her parents and get home. This time, we kept it simpler and went to the Burger King on post, which was right down the road from our barracks.

After we ate, we all hugged each other and said our goodbyes. I told Crystal to call me whenever she wanted to hang out again.

"I sure will," she said.

A couple of days later, I did get a call from her, but she sounded distant. I was doing all the talking. I asked what was the matter. She said there was nothing wrong, but that she was just tired from work. I had a feeling that perhaps she and Steve were talking again. This was almost the same reaction that I had received from her when she broke up with me the previous year. I didn't say anything this time. I just said, "Have a good one and get a hold of me sometime."

"Will do, Nate," she replied. "You take care of yourself."

This time, I didn't bother to dwell on it. This time around, we were friends having good times together.

CHAPTER 4

Four Years and Some News

Since the last day that I had seen Crystal in that Burger King parking lot, over two months had gone by. I had recently been put on orders to be stationed in Korea for a year. My report date was February of '97. I wrote about this tour in my books *Division* and *Lifer*. My last big "hoorah" in this unit was a month-long deployment to Panama that our company had been put on orders for. Back in those days, in the 82nd Airborne, it was common to get sent to Panama as part of either a quick reactionary force, jungle training, or both. I also wrote about this deployment in the same previous books.

Over two months had gone by since Crystal contacted me. Then, one evening I got a call from her.

"Hello, this is Nate."

"Hi, Nate, it's me, Crystal."

"Oh my, it's been a while; how have you been?"

She didn't even try to beat around the bush with me. "Are you ready for this Nate?" she asked me.

"I guess. What's up? Or what's wrong? I can tell by your tone that something is wrong," I said. I could almost guess what she was about to tell me.

"Well, Nate, I'm pregnant, and you're the father."

I immediately thought: "how?" I knew that she was on birth control before, when we dated for two months a year prior. Apparently, she wasn't anymore. I asked her that very question, and she had admitted to me that she had gotten off of birth control for whatever reasons. I didn't know, nor did she tell me. I asked the next major question.

"Okay, Crystal, are you sure that I am the father?"

She paused for a few seconds. "Yes, Nate. You're the only one that I have been with for some time now."

I had to ask. "What about Steve?"

"Nate, I haven't been with him for the past few months now. You've been the only guy I have been with since we last broke up; that I can promise you."

"Okay, what do we do now?" I asked calmly. "I mean, if we move forward with this, I guess we should do a DNA test just so that I know it is my child."

I know she didn't want to hear it, but you have to understand my situation. I was with this girl for two months. She broke up with me abruptly, almost out of nowhere. She contacted me a year later to hang out a couple of times, and now over two months since she'd last seen me, was telling me she was pregnant with my child. It was a lot for me to take in. We remained calm with one another throughout our conversation. That was one thing about Crystal and me, throughout the entire time that we'd known each other, there was never any hostility between us. When we ended the phone conversation, we were both in agreement about a DNA test. I was going to contact the Fort Bragg main hospital because my friends in the barracks told me that they would do DNA testing for the soldiers and their significant others. I would just have to make an appointment, which I was prepared to do. Crystal had told me that she would get back with me when she could coordinate time away from work to be able to drive down to Fort Bragg. I was told that the test could only be conducted on certain days of the week, between

Monday through Friday. Trust me, there were a lot of soldiers going through the same kind of thing.

I waited to hear back from her, but the phone call never came. Every day after work, I would check my answering machine, and there would be nothing from Crystal, no message, no additional information. I continued to do my daily duties in the Army, waiting to hear from her. I had thought about contacting Bridget to see if she had heard from Crystal, but I didn't have Bridget's number either. My friends continued to ask me about it, and I would tell them the same thing—haven't heard from her. "Well then, don't worry about it. Apparently, it isn't your kid," is what I was continuously told in the weeks after she told me. It still dwelled on my mind as I continued to go about my career in the military. We all continued going a hundred miles an hour every day in the life of the 82nd Airborne Division. I never heard from Crystal ever again.

A couple of months went by, and we did our month deployment to Panama. Shortly after, I cleared and signed out of the 82nd Airborne to go on a month of well-needed leave back up to Michigan before my year-long tour in South Korea. It was a great month off from the Army. I stayed a few days with my family in Portage, and then I would drive across the state to stay with my high school friends who I grew up with in my original hometown. My parents had to move across the state of Michigan shortly after I went into the Army due to the facility my dad worked at closing down. So, they had moved to the western part of the state where he had been offered a position at another facility.

When I was with my friends where I grew up, we would go out to the local bars, hang out, and party like we used to do in high school. It was a great time in our lives. We were all in our early twenties and mostly single. I had one or two friends who had gotten married, but their wives were cool too. They were friends from our high school days as well. During that timeline, we would go bowling at our local bowling alley, which was pretty large. After we would bowl a few games, we would go to the sports bar that was connected to the back.

It was new at the time and booming. They had a huge bar, music, a couple of pool tables, and a couple of dart boards. It was fun as hell. You could also run into anybody you went to school with. It was one of the best places that they had built in my hometown. Every time we went there, it was like a class reunion.

Now, there was one bartender who I found very attractive. She was absolutely gorgeous. She was twenty-one years old with long, straight, dark hair. I made it my business to get to know her. The friends I was staying with would have to work during the day but would leave me their house key, and I would go back to that sports bar to visit her. She worked more days than she did nights. She was nice and talkative with me. We would sit there and talk for at least two hours almost every day I was there. Eventually, I asked her if she had been seeing anybody. She was dating a guy who was almost thirty.

"He must make good money," I told her.

"He does pretty good for himself," she replied.

Eventually, I would visit her frequently enough that she would leave the bar and play darts with me. We were getting close, but she had that damn boyfriend. I didn't push her to go against her relationship with him, but God knows I wanted to. After a couple of weeks of me seeing her as often as I could at the bar, I was convinced that she too had an interest in me. We at least had a definite trustworthy friendship.

My time on leave before Korea was getting down to only a few days. I was going to be away for an entire year before I could come back to see her again. The last time I was at the bar visiting her, I told her that I was going to Korea for a whole year and that this was going to be the last time I could see her before I left. So, I asked her for her phone number. She refused to give it to me due since she was in a relationship. I told her that I understood. At that point, I laid it on thick to her that I was attracted to her and that I truly wanted to be in contact with her while I was out of the United States. So, I asked her if I could at least have her address, so that I could write to her. Remember, this was before cell phones and easily accessible internet. These were the days where you had to write a letter on paper, put it into an envelope, put a stamp on it, and put it into the mail. She gave into my request and wrote down her address on a piece of paper.

"Here you go, Nate," she said as she handed it to me. "I'm sorry I didn't give you my phone number, but that's not right for me to do since I'm seeing somebody."

I told her I understood. At least she kept her integrity, and I told myself how lucky this guy must have been to have such a beautiful and honest girl like her. Her name was Lisa, and she eventually became my second wife.

A whole year went by, and now it was March of '98. Again, I had taken thirty days of leave once I returned to the United States and my hometown. One of the first places I went to after spending a few days with my family, was back to the sports bar. I was so hoping to see Lisa working there, even though I had written to her twice while I was in Korea, but never got a letter back.

When I walked in, I turned and headed straight up to the bar. I ordered a beer and nonchalantly asked the bartender, who I didn't recognize, if she still worked there. He asked me who I was talking about. I described her and told him that she had been mostly the day bartender a year ago.

"Oh, her," he said. "No, she doesn't work here anymore. She quit almost a year ago."

That meant that she must have left shortly after I left for overseas duty.

"Well, do you know where she works now, by any chance?" I asked him.

"No. I don't know anything about her. I barely know who you are talking about."

I drank my beer, left the bar, and drove over to my buddy's house, where I was staying at the time. A couple of weeks later, I arrived back at Fort Bragg and back into the 82nd Airborne Division. At that point, I was convinced and even told myself that I would never see her again.

Returning back to Bragg was like going back home, as far as being in the Army goes. The lifestyle hadn't changed a bit. Daily life was go-go-go twenty-four-seven. I had more responsibilities this time around, however. I was assigned as a rifle squad leader and was in charge of eight soldiers. We had field exercise after field exercise. Jumping out of airplanes all the time. Deploying to Fort Polk, Louisiana, et cetera, et cetera. After six months of being there this time around, it was time for our unit to go on two weeks of block leave. It was awesome, because I felt as if I just came off of thirty days of leave in Michigan. The reality was it had been six months ago. We were always working and moving at such a rate of speed all the time that it seemed like yesterday. Anyway, I packed up my clothes, and headed back up to Michigan where my family and friends were.

By this time, it was around the end of September of '98. Again, after seeing and staying with my parents and little brother for a few days, I headed back to my hometown to visit my good friends from high school. This time, I was staying mostly with my buddy John. He had his own house that he had bought from his mother. It was a small house, but a hell of a bachelor's pad. One of the best parts of staying with John was that there was an awesome bar and grill practically across the street from his house. It was my hometown's famous Michael's Roadhouse. It was an awesome place to hang out. Just like before, it was guaranteed that you would run into people you knew from high school. They always had a live band or a DJ on weekends.

John and I were there one Friday night, talking to some old friends up at the bar. All of a sudden, I felt a tap on the shoulder. When I turned around, there was a familiar looking girl smiling at me.

"Hey, what's up? Can I help you?" I asked.

She was a pretty girl, with short, dark hair. There was definitely something familiar about her.

"Is your name Nathan by any chance?" she asked loudly, over the sound of the band playing behind her.

"Yeah, do we know each other?" I asked.

"Kind of. It's been a while, but I'm Lisa from the old sports bar next to the bowling alley."

It hit me immediately who she was. She did look a little different because of her shorter hair. Before, she had long, straight hair. Don't get me wrong; she was still beautiful.

"Oh my God! I'm so sorry that I didn't recognize you at first. You have shorter hair now. Wow! How are you, Lisa? It's so good to run into you again."

I didn't give her a chance to speak at first. As I was running off at the mouth, she just stood there smiling at me. I continued on with, "I got back from Korea over six months ago, and one of the first places I went to was the sports bar looking for you, but they told me you didn't work there anymore."

"Yeah," she said. "I was having issues with the managers, so I quit and am now working at the Dodge dealership in town here."

"Good for you!" I yelled out over the loud music.

I stood up almost awkwardly, leaned over to her and gave her the biggest hug like I found my best friend from twenty years ago. She hugged me back. She was there with some coworkers from the dealership. I could tell that she was feeling a little tipsy from drinking. I didn't care; so was I. I asked her if she wanted to go out and dance with me, and she did. We danced to a couple of songs and then sat back down together. I bought her a drink while we talked for about a half hour nonstop. I did ask her why she never wrote me back when I was in Korea. At least she was honest and said that she was sorry, but she was seeing that guy at the time and didn't think that it would be appropriate. Of course, I bought into it and blew it off. I was just happy that I found her, or more so, she found me. I think I was happier that she came up to me first.

She didn't stay long after that, but before she left, I asked her for her phone number. Lo and behold, she wrote it down and gave it to me without hesitation. Now I had full contact with her. I immediately pulled out my wallet, folded up the piece of paper, and put it away nice and neat. I asked her why she had to leave so soon. She told me that she had been there for quite some time, and that she had to be at work the next morning. We gave each other a hug again and said goodbye. I told her that I was going to call her that next day, and she said, "Okay. That sounds good." I was so excited for the remainder of the evening. I went back to hang out with John and some other friends. Of course, it was time for me to celebrate, so I ordered us all some shots of tequila.

We left the bar and walked back to John's house. I was telling him all about how and when I met Lisa. He told me that he slightly remembered her from the sports bar, and he also agreed that she was a good-looking girl.

"You going to hook up with her before you go back to the Army?" he asked me.

"Oh, yeah, buddy. I'm going to call her around three or four tomorrow after she gets home from work."

Afterall, I had my truck. So, dinner and a movie sounded realistic to me. Maybe afterward, we could go out to Michael's again for some more dancing and drinks. Maybe, just maybe, she would go back and stay with me at John's house. The possibilities were endless. These were all the wishes I had before I went to sleep.

That next morning John and I went out to eat breakfast and then drove around to visit some of our other friends from high school. It was a good day, but when it came time for me to call Lisa, I made sure that I was near a phone. I didn't care if it was back at John's or wherever we were at. I pulled her number out of my wallet and dialed. It was probably one of the most disturbing and disappointing phone calls I had ever made. I asked her if she wanted to go out to dinner and maybe a movie with me, and she said no. I was almost in a state of shock.

"Why not, if you don't mind me asking?"

"Well, I'm kind of seeing somebody right now," she said apologetically.

"What? What about last night? I mean, we danced and talked. We even hugged each other a couple of times."

"I know. I'm sorry, Nate, but I was kind of drunk last night and not thinking clearly. I hope I didn't give you the wrong impression."

"Actually, you did. I mean, you came up to me first and made me feel like you were really interested in me."

At that point, I realized that it was coming off as begging. So, I stopped trying to reason with her. "It's all good, Lisa. I'll let you go and let you get back to your day."

"Okay. Sorry, again, Nate."

We hung up, and that was it. I went back over to John.

"So, what's up, Natedawg? You going out with her tonight or what?" John asked.

"Hell, no dude. She said she can't because she's seeing somebody."

"Don't worry about it, dude. You can hook up with somebody else while you're home," he said.

He didn't understand the point. It wasn't about me trying to hook up with any girl while I was home; I was interested in maybe starting a relationship with this girl.

Nine months passed and my unit was in the middle of the Mojave Desert in California. We were deployed there for a month at the National Training Center for desert warfare training. Originally, it was established for heavy infantry and armor units. Back in the '90s, they would send light units like ours about every other year.

It was June of '99, and it was a hot and miserable summer out there. It was so hot that we could hardly train during the day. Not because we were weak, but because of the heat casualty risk. We already had a soldier suffer from a heat stroke, and he was sent to the Fort Irwin hospital, right into the intensive care unit. So, the whole time we were in our combat operations training, the leadership of our company ordered that we hunker down underneath our poncho hootches that we had set up for shade and drink plenty of water.

The three other squad leaders from our platoon and I snapped our ponchos together, making the ultimate hootch. We sat underneath it for most of the day. We got bored but found ways to entertain ourselves. We played cards, talked, and laughed, and came up with the "name game." You went in order and each person had to name a famous person, first name and last. When it got to the next person, the first name of his famous person would have to start with the last letter of the last name from the previous. For instance, I would say Paul Newman, and the next person could say Neil Diamond.

One afternoon, I was sitting there under the hootch, pulled out my wallet, and began going through it. I was cleaning it out, getting rid of the old stuff I had had in it for years, including old phone numbers of girls. As I was going through it, I came across Lisa's number that she gave me almost a year prior. I was debating whether or not to get rid of it, since she had blown me off twice before. Now the thing was that we were going on block leave as soon as we were to get back to North Carolina. I told my buddies that I was going to try one more time to hook up with her when I got back to Michigan in a couple of weeks. My one buddy called me crazy.

"Isn't that the girl back in your hometown who keeps blowing you off every time you go home?" he asked me.

"Yeah, that's her, but they say the third time's the charm. I'm going to try to hook up with her one more time, and if it doesn't work this time, I'll get rid of her phone number for good."

"You do what you gotta do, but I think you're making a big mistake."

I remember thinking to myself, "What the hell do you care who I call when I'm home on leave?" Whatever. I was going to do my own thing and not worry about what others thought.

A couple weeks later, I was on my way back up to Michigan. I don't know, but I decided to fly up there instead of driving my little truck. My goal this time was to stay mostly with my friends in my hometown and have my parents drive to come visit me. That was convenient for all of us, since my parents had all of their families on that side of the state anyway. So, I would meet them for visits and dinners while I stayed with a buddy of mine, one of my best friends who also was in the

Army for four years. He was out by this time and worked at a nearby factory. He was a bachelor, living in his own little condo in the next town over from where we grew up. It was around the Fourth of July of '99. We hung out with other friends for a couple nights, went out to some nightclubs in nearby Flint, and partied like guys do in their mid-twenties. I had just turned twenty-six.

It was the day after the fourth. I pulled out my wallet and asked my buddy if I could use his phone for a long-distance call.

"Yeah, sure. Go ahead and call," he said. "Who are you trying to hook up with?" he asked. He immediately knew by looking at my face who it was going to be. "What? You still trying to hook up with that Lisa chick? Dude, she's just going to turn you down again."

"I don't care," I replied. "I'm still going to try one more time."

He just laughed at me. For all I knew, she might not even live at the same number anymore.

She answered the phone, "Hello."

"Is this Lisa?" I asked.

"Yes, it is."

"Hey, this is Nathan from the Army."

"Oh, hi, how are you?"

"Good. I'm back in Michigan, staying with my buddy in Davison. I was wondering if we could finally go out sometime while I'm home on leave? Or do you still have a boyfriend?"

"No, we broke up a few months ago. I'm single."

It was music to my ears. "Well, how about dinner with me tonight?" I excitedly asked.

She disappointedly responded with, "Sorry. Unfortunately, I'm not feeling good today. We had a big party last night on the lake for the Fourth of July. They blew off fireworks, and we drank all night."

"Okay, Lisa. I understand. Can I at least give you my buddy's phone number so that you can call when we can go out?"

"Sure. Let me get something to write on." We paused. She came back to the phone and asked what it was. I gave it to her, but I wasn't confident about her ever calling me back, knowing her past of letting me down.

When I got off the phone, Matt was laughing at me.

"Dude! I told you she was going to blow you off again. You never listen to anybody, man!"

I laughed, too, and I made up my mind that that was going to be the last time I would ever attempt to contact her.

"C'mon man," he said. "Let's get cleaned up and go to the bar to play some pool and some darts. We can hook up with a couple of chicks there from high school."

"All right," I said to him.

At that moment, when I went to the spare room to get some new clothes from my bag, his phone rang. Matt answered. "Oh, yeah. He's right here; here you go."

I grabbed the phone from him, and it was her, calling me back. "Hey! What's up Lisa?"

"Well, even though I'm a little hungover today, would you like to come over and hang out at our pool? We're just lounging around, having a few beers, and relaxing. I figured I'd call and see if you wanted to join us, and maybe go out tomorrow night perhaps?" It was freaking music to my ears! I didn't even hesitate to say yes. She said, "Okay great. Here's my address."

Matt told me that I could take his truck. He congratulated me and said that he was happy for me. I knew just what I was going to wear. A nice pair of shorts and a tank top. However, before I would get into the shower, I would have to grab Matt's curl bar with weights and knock out three sets of curls. Then I knocked out three sets of shoulder lifts. If I was going to see this girl again, I had to get my arms a little pumped up first. It was a "dude in his mid-twenties" thing.

When I pulled into her driveway, I had to make sure that I had the correct address, because this looked like a family house. What I mean is, it was a double-story home with a two-car garage. There were a couple of SUVs in the driveway. I thought that maybe she was renting this with a couple of friends. At this time, she would have been around twenty-three. I said to myself, "There's no way that she still lives with her parents." I would soon find out that she did. As a matter of fact, she lived with her parents and two little sisters. I had shown up to a family home. I was already nervous seeing her, let alone her whole family too. Here I was wearing a tank top, I had tattoos up and down my arms and earrings in my left ear—four hoops. I know that these days, that is no big deal, but back in those days, in a conservative little farm town in Michigan, it was.

She walked out to the driveway to meet me. As I got out of Matt's truck, her mouth dropped.

"Hi. How are you?" she asked. "You are Nate, right?"

"Of course," I said. "Has it been that long since we've seen each other?"

"Well, the last time I saw you, it was always wintertime. I didn't know you had tattoos or earrings."

"Oh, yeah," I said. "I also have been shaving my head bald for the past year now."

"What's that all about?" she asked.

"Well, my hair was thinning on top to the point that I just started shaving it completely bald."

She was looking at me with almost a look of disgust in her face. I wasn't feeling it. I almost got back into the truck and left to go back to Matt's. I did ask her about the house, and that's when she broke it down to me that she still lived at home with her family.

"Oh, great," I said. If I would have known that I was going to meet your parents, I would have dressed a little more appropriately."

"No, you're fine," she said. "I was just a little shocked that you look so different than when I knew you before." She was trying to assure me that my appearance was fine with her, but deep down, I knew that she was nervous introducing me to her family. "Come on, let me introduce you to everyone. They're all out back at the pool."

Now I was really nervous.

When we went through her house, she took me to the back patio, where there was a big deck around an above-ground pool. There, her parents were sitting around a table. They had her aunt and uncle over swimming and having a great summer day. Everyone was laughing, joking, and teasing each other. Her uncle was doing cannonballs into the pool. I started relaxing more at that point. Her mom and dad said hi to me. They both stood up and shook my hand and introduced themselves to me. Then her dad asked me the ultimate question: "Hey would you like a beer?" .

At that point, I felt completely relaxed.

"Sure, sir," I replied.

He reached down to his cooler and pulled me out an original Budweiser.

"All we have is Budweiser, I hope that's okay with you, young man."

Of course, I said it was fine. What was I supposed to do, say no to the man? Honestly, at that age, I didn't care what kind of beer I drank. Her mom told me to sit down with them. She even offered me some wine that she happened to be drinking.

"No, ma'am," I said. "The beer is fine. Plus, I have to drive back to Davison. So, I better watch how much I drink today."

I was trying to show them that I was a responsible young adult. She looked at me and laughed and said that Chris (Lisa's dad) always picked up two tall boys to drink on his way home from work every day. At that point, I truly felt relaxed now. All I needed to do now was to get Lisa to talk to me. Her mom's name was Cindy, and at that point, I was feeling more comfortable talking to her mom and dad than I was talking to her. They asked me where I was from in Michigan, where I graduated high school, what I did in the Army, where I was stationed, etc. I explained it all to them, and they seemed happy to hear that I was from the same town, just on the opposite side. They also liked the fact that I was stationed in North Carolina, because Cindy explained to me that they had once had a timeshare for a couple of years just off the coast of North Carolina. I told her that I knew where it was, and that my friends and I had partied there on several weekends. Let's just say that we were hitting it off.

After about my third beer with them, Lisa finally spoke to me and asked if I wanted to go for a ride around the lake with her on their pontoon boat. Her mom answered for me.

"There you go," she said. "You two go out and spend some time alone together. Don't let us take up all of your visit."

I couldn't believe that it could get much better than this. Her parents were telling us to go out alone. Then again, she was in her twenties. It wasn't like we were teenagers going to the homecoming dance or prom. Her dad handed me a couple of beers for the trip around the lake. They were the coolest people and parents that I had ever met.

Once we were on the lake, it was almost like we were back up on the patio. She wasn't talking to me at all. I said to myself, "Oh well. I'll sit here and look at the beautiful scenery around this good size lake and enjoy these Budweiser beers that her dad gave me." I did try to strike up a couple of conversations with her as she drove us around the lake, but her answers were short and simple.

When we pulled up to the dock after the ride around the lake, I helped her tie off the pontoon. All I could think about was to say goodbye to her parents, to her, and then hit the road. As we walked back onto the patio, her mom had asked me to stay for dinner; they were cooking steaks on the grill. I very much wanted to, but Lisa was making me uncomfortable by ignoring me.

"Oh, no. I need to get my buddy's truck back to him but thank you so much for the offer and your hospitality."

They both stood up again and shook my hand and told me to come back to visit anytime. I assured them that I would. In reality, I was telling myself that there would be no chance in hell of me returning to that house or even contacting Lisa ever again. She walked me to Matt's truck, we gave each other a little tap-tap hug and said goodbye to each other. I did tell her thank you for the invite, and that I had a really great time. I also told her that I thought her parents were awesome.

About twenty minutes later, I arrived back at Matt's. When I walked into his place, he was sitting on his couch with a girl. He introduced me to her, and I apologized for interrupting them.

"Not at all, brother. Grab yourself a beer out of the fridge and sit down. I want to hear all about your visit that I thought was going to be a little longer."

The girl on the couch with him was one of his neighbors. She was good looking too. I remember thinking how lucky this dude was.

As I was explaining the visit I had at Lisa's, Matt's phone rang.

"I'll get it for you, Matt. You guys just relax," I said.

"Hi, is Nate there, please? This is Lisa."

"This is Nate. I just got back to my friend's place; is everything all right?" I thought that maybe I forgot my sunglasses over her place or something.

"Yes and no," she said. "What I mean is, I wanted to apologize for the way I acted this afternoon."

I played stupid. "What do you mean? I had a great time."

"No, you didn't. It's okay, you don't have to lie, but I appreciate it. My mom and dad told me how I was acting, being all silent toward you and all. It's just that today I am so hungover from last night's Fourth of July party we had at the lake. As a matter of fact, when I get off the phone with you, I'm going inside to lay on the couch and take a nap."

"It's all right," I said. "I completely understand. I've been there and done that many times."

"Nate, would you like me to pick you up tomorrow after I get out of work, and take you out to dinner?"

I couldn't believe this was happening. "Absolutely," I said. "What time do you think you'll be around?"

She told me the time, and she knew where Matt's condo was. It was all set after that. I got off the phone with her and explained everything that had just occurred to Matt and his neighbor. Matt advised me to go out with her the next night and to take it from there.

She picked me up early the next evening, and we went out to dinner. Afterward, we went back to Matt's and had a few drinks. We went outside to smoke a cigarette. After we smoked our cigarettes, we began talking. I was just drunk enough where I started laying it on thick to her. I told her how I felt about her all these past couple of years, ever since I met her when she was a bartender. I then leaned over and kissed her on the mouth. She grabbed the back of my head, and there we were, making out on my friend's porch. We spent every night together after that, partying over at Matt's and getting to know one another. She even drove me to the airport when it was time for me to fly back to North Carolina. At that point, it was safe to say that we were officially boyfriend and girlfriend.

Back in my barracks room, I called her that evening when I arrived to tell her that I made it back safe and sound. It was a promise she asked me to do for her when I was back in my room. We must have talked an hour every night. From that point on, every long weekend, holiday, and any time we were given away from the Army, I would drive back home to Michigan and spend the entire time with her and her family. We spent Thanksgiving together at her aunt and uncle's house and Christmas at her house with her parents and sisters. We would drive back and forth to my parents' house to celebrate the holidays with them as well.

Lisa and I had a plan to move in together down in Fayetteville, North Carolina. We were going to rent a house or an apartment. I had even started looking around nice neighborhoods. There were always homes for rent in that area around Fort Bragg. Soldiers were always coming and going on a weekly basis. At the time, I was a staff sergeant, and she was going to get a job as soon as she got down there. Her supervisor at the Dodge dealership she was working at back home had already planned on giving her a good reference. So, she would have no problem doing the same thing down in Fayetteville. One thing was for sure, there were plenty of dealerships outside of Fort Bragg. Therefore, we weren't going to have any problems with affording to have our own place. Single soldiers were doing it all the time. The difference between living off post as a single soldier and off post as a married soldier was that if you were single, you had to pay out of your own pocket. The Army wasn't going to pay you additional housing allowances as they do for married soldiers with families.

It was the eve of her packing up her stuff and moving down when she called me with some bad news. Her parents would not give their consent for her living with a guy outside of marriage. I didn't understand. She was twenty-three years old. What consent did she need? I even told her that they would eventually get over it and that this wasn't 1955.

"How are they against us living together when they've been allowing me to sleep with you in your bed every time I've come home for the past several months?" I asked.

She agreed and disappointedly replied back with, "I know Nate. It's actually more of my mom's opinion because of her family's Catholic beliefs. It would be an embarrassment for her to have to tell my grandparents, aunts and uncles."

I couldn't believe what I was hearing. Her parents seemed to be the coolest parents that I had ever met, up until I heard this. I was allowed to sleep with her every time I went back up to Michigan to visit.

After we hung up, I sat there on my couch dumbfounded. I reached over to my little refrigerator, grabbed myself a beer, sat back on the couch, and lit up a cigarette. I sat there contemplating and contemplating some more. The more beer I had, the more my decision was becoming clearer. I knew what I needed to do if I were to be with this girl. The next day, I went to the Fayetteville mall with one of my buddy squad leaders and bought an engagement ring.

When I went back to be with her for Christmas, her mom explained to me more in depth of why her family would disapprove of her living with a guy, especially out of state. Furthermore, they were also concerned about her not having medical insurance, due to her still being under her dad's. Her being out of the state of Michigan would mean that she wouldn't qualify for it anymore. I assured her that I completely understood and agreed. What she didn't know, just like the rest of them, was that I was going to propose to her Christmas morning after we exchanged gifts. I did just that. After the gift exchange, I took a pillow from the couch, reached into my pocket, and knelt down in front of Lisa. I opened up the box.

"Will you marry me?" I asked.

She put her hand over her mouth and said yes. We both stood up and hugged and kissed each other. Her mom, dad, and sisters were going ballistic in their living room. I had shocked the whole family. They were all surprised and happy. Her dad walked over to a cupboard in the kitchen and pulled out a bottle of champagne and some glasses. He poured each of us a glass, and we toasted to our new engagement. That was Christmas morning of '99.

Two days later, I had to drive back to Fort Bragg. Man, those were long drives back and forth, back and forth. It was about a twelve-hour drive one way from Fayetteville to my hometown. I did it all the time during the '90s. I was young, so it was easy for me. I would only stop two, maybe three times each way to fill up on gas, fill up my coffee mug, and I'd be on my way again. It was too easy.

Back at Bragg, I had some responsibilities to take care of, like looking for a place to live. I drove around for a couple of days looking but didn't find anything that interested me. One of the soldiers in my platoon suggested I come look at the place he and his wife lived at. So, I did. They were two-story condos about twenty to twenty-five minutes from our barracks, which wasn't bad at all. They were nice, with two bedrooms, two full baths, and a full kitchen with all appliances, including a dishwasher. A dishwasher already installed in the '90s was a big deal. We had a little patio out back, with a little storage shed. It was just under $800 a month, and I was immediately sold. I went and talked to the manager of the complex, he showed me an empty one that was for rent, and I jumped on it. I had enough money saved up to go ahead and pay for my first and last month's rent. I signed the contract with the manager, and it was a done deal.

That evening I called Lisa and told her all about it. She was so excited. I could hear her parents in the background asking her about it. She would talk to me and then tell them all about the condo. It was an exciting time for us all. The only thing I had to do now was find some furniture, which was always easy to do around any military installation. A squad leader buddy of mine from our platoon was getting rid of his couch and loveseat. The set was in great condition. He said his wife wanted a leather set, and that was why they were getting rid of it. I bought it off of him for a hundred bucks. He even helped me load them up and carry them into my new place. Now all I needed was a kitchen table and some chairs. A bedroom set was no problem, because we were going to have hers that she had in Michigan. Once we were married, the Army would hire movers to pick it up and deliver it to our place in Fayetteville. I went to the Fort Bragg Post Exchange (PX) and bought a kitchen set, a coffee table, end table, and lamp for the living room. I put it all on my PX credit card and figured she and I would have it paid off in a couple of months, no problem. Now, all there was to do was go back up to Michigan and get married.

I flew up there with the intent of driving back in her car. Everything was falling into place. I had our house already set up and ready to go, minus the groceries, of course. The administrative section of my unit already had my paperwork ready to go for off-post housing allowance and her being my dependent, which would put her automatically on health insurance, including dental and optical. All I needed to give them was a marriage certificate to add to the paperwork, and it was a done deal. A lot of people do not realize that the military truly does take care of its families.

On January 16, 2000, I married my second wife after dating each other for six months. We kept it simple and cheap. We were married by the justice of the peace in our hometown. Afterward, her parents hosted a party for us back at their house. All of our close family and friends were there. There was plenty of food, music, dancing, and booze. It was a great time. When the party was over, we left and drove to town. We had ourselves a nice suite reserved at the Best Western hotel. Our wedding night went off without a hitch.

CHAPTER 5

Newlyweds with a Major Surprise

I was only on a four-day weekend pass when we got married. So, we had to get on the road and head down to North Carolina. It was a cold and snowy Michigan winter day when we left her mom and dad's. We had her gray Dodge Intrepid packed with as much of her stuff as we could get in it. We said goodbye to everybody, gave our hugs, and we pulled out of the driveway. I looked at Lisa.

"You are about to embark on a great adventure," I said. She just looked at me and smiled. We were heading south.

A few months had gone by, and it was early spring of 2000, around the end of March. The Carolina weather was beautiful outside, we were doing great, and Lisa was making friends with some of my friends' wives. I was getting ready to attend the Advanced Airborne School, or Jumpmaster School, as most refer to it as. Everything was falling into place. Lisa and I had also recently found out that we were expecting our first baby.

We were sitting on the couch one evening watching television when the phone rang. My wife answered it, and it was a woman on the other end, asking for me.

"May I ask who this is? Nathan is my husband," said Lisa.

I looked up at Lisa, concerned. I reached out and she handed me the phone. It was a cordless phone, so I got off the couch and paced around the living room while I answered.

"Hello, this is Nate."

"Hello, Nate," said the woman. "I'm calling you from Durham. I got your number from the Fayetteville operator."

"Okay, what can I do for you?" I asked.

I didn't know who the heck this person was. My wife was sitting there with her arms crossed as if I was up to something.

"Do you remember a girl named Crystal from Durham?"

"Yes, I dated a girl named Crystal about four or five years ago, and yes, she was from Durham. Why, what's up?"

"Well, Nathan, I'm a friend and coworker of Crystal's."

The suspense had my mind racing. I looked at Lisa and shrugged. I didn't know where this phone call was going.

"Okay, what can I help you with?"

"Nathan, this isn't easy for me to tell you, and Crystal doesn't even know that I'm speaking to you about it, but you have a little boy here in Durham. He's a little over three or maybe just turned four, but you do have a son."

"Wow," I said to her. "That's quite some unexpected news. You know this because Crystal told you?"

"Yes, I've known and have worked with her for quite some time now. I knew about it when she was pregnant with him."

All of this was rushing through my head at a speed that I cannot explain. I was going back through time in my head, trying to remember timelines and details of the last time that I spoke to her on the phone. I did remember her telling me she was pregnant, and that was the last time we had spoken to one another. Since I never heard back from her again, I assumed that either she wasn't pregnant, or if she were, that the child wasn't mine. All of this was running through my mind. I thought about it and remained silent.

"Are you still there, Nathan?"

"Yes, ma'am, I am. I'm just trying to take this all in. Can I ask why you are telling me this and not Crystal?" I asked with concern.

"Either she didn't want you to know, or she was ashamed for not telling you all of these years."

I thought about it and it didn't matter why she hadn't said anything to me; either way, this was the first time that I was hearing about it.

"Nathan, she doesn't expect anything from you, or want anything, either. Like I said, she doesn't even know that I'm telling you this. I just thought that it was the right thing to do, to tell you that you have a son here in Durham."

I didn't know what to believe. For all I knew, Crystal was sitting next to her while she was on the phone with me. Having been in the Army for ten years, I had seen a lot of broken-up relationships. Especially around Fort Bragg.

"I can mail you some pictures that I have of him, if you would like. That way you can make up your own mind about how you would like to pursue this, or if you even want to pursue this any further at all. I just thought it was my moral obligation to tell you."

Some friend, I thought. If Crystal didn't want her to say anything, she sure was doing a bad job of it. I thought about it and immediately told her yes, that I would like to see some pictures of him. I asked her if Crystal was still with the same boyfriend. I couldn't remember his name at that point. She told me that she was, and that they had another child together as well. She also told me that he knew that my boy wasn't his, but it didn't matter to him, that he was raising him as his own.

I gave her my address, so that she could mail me the pictures. Household internet had just come around, and we had just gotten our first desktop computer with internet, but it was dial-up service. This meant that you plugged your hard drive into a phone jack on the wall, and you had to wait sometimes several minutes before you were signed into the internet. There was no such thing as high-speed internet in those days. My wife and I wouldn't even have our first cell phones until three years later.

I gave her my address in Fayetteville, and she gave me her phone number in order for me to reach her. She didn't offer to give me Crystal's, nor did I ask or even want it. Imagine being a newlywed and having to tell your spouse that you may or may not have a child with someone else. Oh, yeah, throw in having an ex-girlfriend's phone number from several years ago, and the fact that you and your newlywed spouse recently found out that the two of you are expecting a new baby as well. All I knew was that it was going to be a long evening full of some serious conversation.

I hung up the phone, sat down next to my wife, and explained the entire story. Not just the phone conversation, but I had to go back to 1995 and explain my short relationship with Crystal. I didn't expect Lisa to get upset, nor did she, because all of this took place long before we had even met. We'd had our share of relationships with other people prior to us being together. Hell, I was even married and divorced by that time as well. Anyway, she took it all in stride, and she completely understood. She also agreed on wanting to see pictures of this child just as much as I did.

The next day I arrived at my unit and immediately told my squad leader buddies about all this news that I had received the night prior. They thought it was funny.

"See how it goes, Natedawg? You play, you have to pay!" They all laughed.

"Well, dudes, it ain't that funny. Number one, I may have a son in Durham that I never knew about. Two, I just got married a few months ago. Three, we're expecting a baby now too."

"Four, wait till you find out you have other kids from Germany and Korea!" they added.

I stood there shaking my head and smiling. I, too, busted out laughing. I couldn't keep a straight face anymore. I would be doing the same thing to these guys, if the shoe were on the other foot.

"So, whatcha gonna do, Natedawg?"

"I'm just going to have to wait until I see these pictures when they arrive in the mail. After that, I'll make up my mind on whether or not I'm going to pursue a DNA test."

About a week later, my wife came in the house with the mail and said that I had a letter from Durham. I grabbed it out of her hand, opened it up, and sat down on the couch. I pulled out the first picture, sat there for a second, and came to my conclusion immediately. The picture of this child looked exactly like my little brother did when he was three or four years old. My little brother and I look identical. We have the same facial appearances, jaw and nose structure, same eyes with the same color, and same hair color. The toddler in the picture looked exactly like he did. He had the same cheeks with little dimples, and his hair color was the same light brown with little curls in the back and sides.

"Well? Let me see, let me see," said Lisa.

I told her to wait a minute, that I was still studying this picture. I really wasn't studying anything, because I was already convinced that he was my child. I then handed it to her as I grabbed the other two out of the envelope. All three pictures were from his birthday party. Knowing the timeline, it would have been his third birthday. All three pictures looked like my little brother.

"Oh, absolutely not. This kid looks nothing like you at all. No. There's no way that he is yours. I think somebody is looking for some child support with three years of back-payments."

She immediately dismissed the entire possibility that this could be my son.

"I don't know, Lisa. In my opinion, he looks identical to my little brother when he was a toddler. I mean, he has the same features, skin tone, smile—everything."

"No way," she said, raising her voice a bit. "That kid looks nothing like you or your brother."

I sat there on the couch for about twenty minutes just staring at all three of these pictures. There was also a short paragraph letter in the envelope as well. I read it, and it had his name and stated that they were pictures of his recent birthday party. I put everything in the envelope and placed it in a drawer in the kitchen.

"Well, what are you going to do now?" Lisa asked.

"Not sure yet. This is a lot for me to take in right now. I'm going to call that woman back sometime this week and get some more information from her."

"Like what?"

Again, her voice was rising. I could tell she was getting agitated with this entire situation. I believe that she was getting more agitated because I had refused to dismiss it as she did. I knew in my heart and mind that dismissing it was not what I was going to do.

"Nathan! I asked you like what? What additional information do you need?"

I told her that I at least needed to get into contact with Crystal. I also told her that I had every intention of getting a DNA test to confirm what I believed to be true. As soon as I told her that, she got angry and started yelling.

"We have a new life together! We are expecting our own child! And you still want to pursue this idea of yours?"

"Lisa, it's not an idea, it's a situation where the truth needs to be confirmed."

"Well, what exactly are you going to do if it is confirmed that it is your child? Are you going to take that boy from his mother and the family that he knows?"

"No! I'm not going to do that at all!" I caught myself getting upset. So, I paused, took a deep breath, and gathered my thoughts. I then said to her calmly, "Look, Lisa. I need to take this one step at a time. What I need to do first is to contact this woman and see if I can get back in touch with Crystal. Then I will go from there. Okay?"

She looked at me and calmly nodded.

"Okay," I said. "C'mon, sweetheart. Let's sit back down in the living room and put it out of our minds tonight. Let's give it a rest for a couple of days, and then I'll call this girl back and try to get in touch with this ex-girlfriend of mine."

Lisa looked down and shook her head. I could tell she was upset, as she should have been. I could admit how delicate this situation truly was.

I showed up at work the next morning, and my buddies were waiting to hear from me.

"Well, Natedawg, did you get your pictures yet?"

I told them I did and that I believed he was my child. They didn't laugh or find it funny at all. Instead, they got serious.

"Okay, now what?"

I told them what my plan was, which was the same thing that I told my wife the night prior. It was going to be a step-by-step plan that I was going to make happen by contacting this girl back in order to get a hold of Crystal. At this point, I had already forgotten Crystal's last name. That's how long it had been since I had contact with her. I couldn't remember any of their last names—Bridget or Erin's either. My buddies advised me to not rush into this situation, but to ease myself into it. Afterall, Crystal had a full family in Durham, and the last thing I wanted to do was disrupt their lives. It was a delicate matter that I needed to treat as such. Delicate not just for their family, but for mine as well.

A couple days had passed by, and it was over two weeks since the woman from Durham had called me with the surprise news. I had decided to not call her at home in front of Lisa, but to do it alone. I didn't want to get her all riled up, especially with her being pregnant. I figured it would be better to call her while I was at work, instead of risking getting the wife upset again. We didn't need the extra tension at home. So, I had asked one of my soldiers in the barracks if I could use his phone in his room and paid him for the long-distance call to Durham. I pulled the woman's number out of my wallet and dialed. It rang twice, and then a series of three beeps came over the phone, followed by a recording that said, "We're sorry, but the phone number you are trying to reach has been disconnected. Please hang up and try again or wait for an operator to come on the line."

I hung up the phone and dialed her number again. It was the same thing. What were the chances of this happening? The lady who told me about this news just had her phone disconnected. I waited for the operator to come on the line as the recording had suggested. That never happened. Instead, the recording continued three times, and then the phone connection would go silent. More questions and scenarios ran through my head. What if she purposely gave me a number that had been disconnected already, or if all of this was just a hoax? I thought about whether or not her return address was on the envelope that the pictures were sent in, which was back home in my kitchen. I figured I'd let it go until I got back home.

When I got home, the first thing I did was give the wife a hug and a kiss and asked her how her day was and how she felt. We had a small conversation, and then I headed to the kitchen, right for the junk drawer that I had put the envelope in. I pulled it out, and there was no return address on it. I felt like I was stuck, helpless, without any way to get in touch with Crystal back in Durham. I even thought about how to get to her house. I was trying to remember what exit to take off of Interstate 40, but I couldn't. I even thought about taking a day, grabbing a buddy of mine, driving to Durham, and then hope that it would all come back to me, and I would remember how to get to her house—if she even still lived there.

My wife came into the kitchen because she heard me slamming the drawer and cursing.

"What's wrong?" she asked.

I explained to her the entire situation—how I tried to contact this friend of Crystal's. She sat there at the table and took it all in.

"I thought she had her return address on this damn thing, but she didn't. So, as of right now, I'm stuck without any way of getting a hold of anybody."

"Well, can you remember Crystal's last name?" Lisa asked.

"No. That's the problem, and the only person who would know other than me would be some girl from Raleigh named Bridget. Hell,

I can't even remember her last name."

As I thought about it, I realized I probably never knew her last name. I think I only knew her as Bridget, and that was it. I wouldn't even know how to get a hold of her ex-boyfriends, because they had left Fort Bragg years ago. I didn't even know if they were still in the Army or not.

Lisa got up from the table, walked over to me, and gave me a hug.

"Nate," she said, looking me in the eyes, "Maybe it's not meant to be. Maybe you're not meant to pursue this any further than what you already have. I told you what I think. I told you that I don't think this boy looks anything like you."

I stood there with a blank stare on my face.

"Maybe you're right," I said. "I don't know. Either way we look at this whole situation, it is frustrating me, and I think it will continue to frustrate me for a long time. Perhaps forever, until I find out for sure."

"Nate, this October, we are going to have a baby. I need you to stay focused on your family here. I know it is bothering you, but in time, you're going to have to figure it out, just how to get over this obsession of finding out what you may not even want to get yourself involved in. You continuing to pursue this issue could cause more harm to this boy's family than perhaps you think. You are getting ready to start Jumpmaster School in a few days. You need to be focusing your full attention on that. You keep telling me that it's going to be one of the most difficult schools you may ever get into while you're in the Army. Now you need to have your complete attention on the next few weeks while you attend school. You owe it to yourself. Let it go, Nate. Let it go. If it is your child—which I am convinced that it is not—obviously, they don't want you to find out for whatever reason. Look at it like this: Do them the favor of not pursuing it anymore."

I looked at her and shrugged, shaking my head in disbelief. I walked into the living room, sat down on the couch, and didn't say a word for the rest of the night. My confirmation of this child being mine wouldn't come for another twenty-four years.

CHAPTER 6

Wondering Throughout the Years

The years went by. I had to leave Fort Bragg to attend US Army Drill Sergeant School in South Carolina. I did end up graduating from Jumpmaster, but right when I was in the middle of the school, I received my notice that I had been selected for drill sergeant duty for a minimum of two years at Fort Jackson, South Carolina. All the details of these events were illustrated in my last book, *Lifer*.

My wife was overdue with our daughter, Madyson. She was due in mid-October, which we were home in Michigan on leave for. The plan was to have our daughter, and then drive down and report to Fort Jackson. She was almost a month overdue. I think about it today and I wonder why the doctor never induced her. Instead, she was pregnant with my daughter for over ten months. Madyson was born in November of 2000 in the same hospital that I was born in back in my hometown. Afterward, we waited about five days and then hit the road back down south. This time was different, though. We weren't going back to Fort Bragg and the 82nd Airborne, but to a new duty station and a lifestyle that I had only heard bad things about—drill sergeant duty.

Fifteen months later, my wife gave birth to my son, Taylor, while I was a year into being in South Carolina as a drill. I must admit, it was a little difficult for me and Lisa. I wasn't home much. Drill sergeant duty was everyday with minimal time off. I had two babies at home that my wife was taking care of by herself. Often, we would have family come down and stay with us for a few days at a time. They would help out with the babies. It was a difficult time, but we made it happen, and we made it as fun as we could. The one good thing about drill sergeant duty was that the two years that I was there, we got to be on leave for the holidays. So, we got to spend Christmas and New Year's back in Michigan while I was stationed there. Yes, the recruits would get what was called Christmas Exodus, which was nothing more than a fancy phrase for Christmas break. Therefore, we drill sergeants would get leave as well. It wasn't like that back at Fort Bragg. Your unit that you were assigned may or may not have block leave during the holidays. The 82nd Command would alternate it by regiments each year—until 9/11 happened. After that tragic day, not only did the world change, but so did the structure of our entire military.

After my time at Fort Jackson was complete, it was back at Fort Bragg for me. This was my third time being stationed in the 82nd Airborne. When it was all said and done, I had spent half of my twenty-year military career in that unit on Ardennes Street at Bragg. Great times. Every now and then, I would think back to that child in Durham and try to imagine what age he would be when he would enter my mind.

During that third tour at Bragg, it was between the years of 2003 to 2006. Our military as a whole was running nonstop, day after day, month after month, and year after year. The Global War on Terrorism ran deep among our units. Within seven or eight months of me returning to Fort Bragg from drill sergeant duty at Fort Jackson, my new unit was sent to Iraq for the first time. They had just returned from a tour in Afghanistan when I arrived back. I thought it sucked being trapped at Fort Jackson being a drill sergeant while units of the 82nd were fighting in Afghanistan. I couldn't wait to get back to North Carolina.

The years went by, and so did my time in the Army. I eventually went to combat with my unit, but not after I had to complete a three-month-long leadership academy at Fort Benning, Georgia. Immediately after, I had to report and attend the US Army Ranger School as well. Upon return to Fort Bragg from there, I was home with my family for about two weeks, and then I was off to link up with my unit in Iraq. In the year of 2003, I may have spent a total of one entire month with my family.

When we got back from the Middle East in spring of 2004, they sent us on block leave for two weeks. We went home to Michigan as usual. However, this time it was different. I was dealing with recent combat memories in my head, going a million miles per hour between field exercises, schools in Georgia, and now—being back home. Everybody was asking me about this and that, and especially about Iraq. I would put on the show by answering their questions and keeping a smile on my face, when all I wanted to do while I was back home was sit at a bar or at a buddy's house drinking beer. At that time in my life, though, I wasn't drinking at all. So, I stayed around and entertained family for the majority of my time home for two weeks.

When we got back to our unit at Fort Bragg, it was back on, as if there never was a deployment at all. We went right back to going one hundred miles per hour every single day. Field training exercises that would last two weeks at a time in the woods and ranges of Fort Bragg. Airborne jumps were integrated within the field exercises as well. What really was happening was that we were gearing up for another combat deployment in the near future, so all we did was train, train, and train some more. This went on for the next year.

By the summer of 2005, my wife had about hit her limit with me being in this environment. Actually, she had about enough of me. I was never home. As a matter of fact, I think I was home more as a drill sergeant than I was since we had returned back to Fort Bragg in early 2003. When I was home, it seemed all we did was become irritated with one another. I was constantly stressed out from my unit.

Even on weekends that we had off, weekends that we weren't in the field, I had to be on edge. As a platoon sergeant, if we had a soldier get into an alcohol-related incident, we would have to pay the price as well. As leaders, we were responsible for everything our soldiers did or failed to do. So, if you weren't stressed about being evaluated on your combat evaluations in the field, you had to constantly worry about one or two of your soldiers getting a DUI back on main post. I had two soldiers in my platoon get a DUI in the past year since we had returned from Iraq. My second soldier caused me to get a letter of concern from our battalion commander. Like I said, they punished us for our subordinates' wrong doings. What the bigger chain of command wasn't seeing was that the more these combat deployments were continuing, along with constant training in the field, the alcohol abuse was increasing throughout the ranks. More soldiers were getting in trouble throughout our battalion on a weekly basis. It was a stressful time for all of us. Within ten months of our unit being back from the Middle East, our battalion had twenty-two DUIs and alcohol-related incidents that were being tracked at the Division Headquarters-level, and at Army-level as well.

By August of 2005, Lisa had filed for divorce up in Michigan. She had both of the kids with her as I remained at Fort Bragg. The next few months were tough. Our unit was gearing up to deploy to Iraq again soon, set to leave that next January of 2006. I was put on orders to change duty stations, this time, to an Army ROTC training battalion up in Northwest Ohio. I had already done enough time at my unit in Fort Bragg, which was three years, so I was given permission to change station, not only by my chain of command, but by the Army as well. It was what I had requested, so that I had an opportunity to be stationed somewhere closer to my son and daughter, who were a couple of hours north in Michigan. If I couldn't stop this divorce from happening, at least I could be part of my children's lives. That was the way I looked at it, and that's what I did. Had they been older, around their teenage years, I would have stayed right where I was at. However, they were toddlers, and it was a crucial time to be part of their lives. They were too young to realize what was going on. All they knew was that Mommy and Daddy weren't together anymore. In January of 2006, I left Fort Bragg, North Carolina for good. I never returned again, except to visit one time a couple of years later.

After my time in Northwest Ohio, I was put on orders to be stationed in Kansas. The deployments to the Middle East were going nonstop, back-to-back for most combat units throughout all of the military. The unit I was assigned to was on orders to deploy to Iraq for a year. I figured it was going to be my last "hoorah" before I was to retire from the Army. I had already made up my mind that I was going to do twenty years and retire. I wanted to be part of my children's lives, which was the reason I left Bragg in the first place.

After a couple of years serving as an ROTC instructor, I had established a new relationship with a beautiful young lady, who had also served a term in the Army. I met her on campus, as she was a student getting ready to graduate. She was an ROTC Cadet within the same program that I was an instructor in. Although I wasn't her direct instructor for her class, it would still be against Army Regulation for me to ask her out. The Army looked at it as fraternization between an instructor and a trainee. Both of us had an interest in one another. We would catch one another from time to time looking at each other from across the room. There simply was a vibe between us.

Once she graduated, she had almost ten months of downtime before her report date to the Basic Officer Leadership Course. She was part of the Army National Guard as a newly commissioned officer from Bowling Green State University Army ROTC. She had volunteered to assist the ROTC's recruitment program. She was excited because while she would be on this temporary assignment, she would be receiving full active duty pay until her report date to her required school in Georgia. At this point, we considered each other coworkers. She was no longer a trainee, but an ROTC cadre member—the same as me.

Once she started this assignment, I asked her out on a date. She said yes, without hesitation. At that point, we were off to dinner together, and then it continued. It wasn't long before we were dating on a regular basis. After a few weeks, we considered ourselves boyfriend and girlfriend. Not long after that, we decided to live together. She moved into my house that I was renting, and we were a serious committed couple. We kept our relationship a secret due to professionalism in the workplace, but furthermore, it was also against regulation for an officer to date an enlisted member. I know, it sounds stupid, and it was. Around the late '90s, the Army came up with a regulation that officers and enlisted members were forbidden to date one another. Before this policy, they could date and have relationships, but the rules were that they had to be in separate units, not under the same chain of command. Therefore, there would be no conflicts of interests within their unit. Other soldiers could complain that there would be favoritism. For example, an enlisted soldier could get away with breaking the rules if perhaps he was dating the officer in charge of him. It was the law of the land within the military. Her name was Jessica, and after about a year of living together, she became my third wife. We are currently married and have been for the past seventeen years. I know, I know: third times a charm, right?

I had been on Facebook since the spring of 2006. It was fairly new at the time and was popular only among the university students across the nation. However, as we all know today, it was growing at an alarming rate. By 2008, I was reconnecting with many of my friends from the past, including soldiers and high school friends. I didn't have much family who had caught on to it yet; I think maybe my brother and a couple of cousins. I was in Iraq for the majority of 2009. So, I had brought my own laptop, and my roommate and I purchased our own internet service from an Iraqi vendor who had his own business on our base, which was in Northwest Baghdad. One evening, I got on Facebook and noticed a familiar name pop up, sending me a friend request. It was my old girlfriend from Raleigh, North Carolina— Erin. I hadn't seen or talked to her in about twelve or thirteen years.

I accepted her request. I know I was married, but I didn't look at it as accepting a friend request from an ex-girlfriend, but like reconnecting with someone from over ten years ago during my youth.

Even after all of those years, the chance of me having a son back there in North Carolina was still on my mind. After all the greetings and pleasantries between myself and Erin, I waited for a couple of days, and finally messaged her about my possible son. Erin never knew or met Crystal, but they both had the same connection with Bridget. If I could get a hold of Bridget, then I knew I could at least get Crystal's full name, and perhaps her address. It was worth a shot for me to ask. I asked Erin about getting a hold of Bridget, and she remembered hearing about the whole situation between me and Crystal, but she hadn't had contact with Bridget for over ten years. She had no way of getting a hold of her. She told me that she didn't even know if she still lived in the state of North Carolina anymore. I accepted her answer, but I was disappointed. I asked her for Bridget's last name, but she couldn't remember it either. She told me that she thought that Bridget had gotten married about ten years prior. I wanted to attempt to find her on Facebook as well. I searched for "Bridget from North Carolina." A few came up, but no profile looked like her.

I returned from Iraq in October of 2009, after thirteen months straight without taking a mid-tour leave. I was quite strung out, but excited at the same time. I was excited to see my wife and kids again after over a year, and I was excited to be getting out of the Army after twenty years of service.

My unit that I was assigned to had seen me off into my retirement with the utmost respect. We were a tight, caring unit that took care of our soldiers when they left. I had a great retirement ceremony. The wife and I were in the middle of building a new house back in the town that we lived in when I was stationed at ROTC in Ohio. It was a little difficult, because we were doing the whole thing over the phone and the internet. We made it happen, though, and it went off with only minimal hiccups.

On April 1, 2010, my wife and I drove out of Fort Riley, Kansas. I looked out my rearview mirror, and not only did I see the sign of Fort Riley but could also visualize driving away from the Army as a whole. We were heading back to Ohio. We both drove our separate vehicles and followed each other the whole way back. It was an easy drive, straight across Interstate 70 to Dayton, Ohio. We then turned north toward Toledo on Interstate75 for about two hours, and that was it.

Our plan was to stay with some friends from our old neighborhood from when our house was being finished by the builders. It was going to take about three weeks, which was perfect, because we were headed up to Michigan to spend a week or so with the kids.

It was a great time in our lives. I was officially out of the Army, and we were moving into our new home that would be our retirement home for good. I had counted how many times I had moved complete households during the past twenty years since I graduated from high school. It came to a total of ten times. In 2010, my wife Jessica and I were done moving and have lived happily in our new home ever since. We have zero intention of ever moving again.

CHAPTER 7

Discovering Another Family

I had been retired for a couple of years, and the wife and I were really enjoying it. I was working on my master's degree, she was (and still is) working for CSX railroad and was serving in the National Guard at the same time. We were enjoying our new house. Even to this day, fourteen years later, I wake up excited and in disbelief that we have our beautiful house. It is a peaceful, quiet life these days compared to the lifestyle of the military.

We did vacations at least once a summer with the kids. Gatlinburg, Tennessee, Louisville, Kentucky, Virginia Beach, and we vacationed once in South Carolina. We stayed in a nice cabin on Weston Lake, Fort Jackson. We were always doing something. We made the most of our time with my son and daughter. There were times where I wanted to and even tried to find out information about my possible son in North Carolina. Since retiring, it had been bothering me more and more. I had more time to think about it since I wasn't going a hundred miles per hour anymore. I attempted again to ask Erin on Facebook if she had contact with Bridget by any chance. I really wanted to find this boy, who by this time would be a teenager. It had been several years since I asked her before, and she said she hadn't had contact with her, but I figured it had been worth a shot. She said she still didn't know anything about Bridget anymore.

Ever since I left the service, I made it clear to my son and daughter that they were welcome to live permanently with me whenever they wanted. To just let me know, and I would work it out with their mother. At this time, I was still getting them every other weekend, holidays, and half the summers. They each had their own bedrooms at our house in Ohio. They also had their friends in Ohio as well. Jess and I were friends with many couples, and their kids were the same age as Maddy and Taylor. So, they were all friends as well. Most of the time when we would go on vacation, one or two other families would go with us, and we would all vacation together. We would either get our own cabins, hotel rooms, or share a condo together. It was a fun time for all of us.

When my daughter entered high school, she asked me to move in with us permanently. My wife and I were so excited.

"Of course, of course!" I told her.

I had wished my son wanted to as well, but he was content staying at his mom's house in Michigan. That was fine. I never tried nor ever wanted to pressure them into leaving their mom's house, after all of these years of them being with her.

I called Lisa and told her about Maddy's request to live in Ohio with Jess and me. She said that she would talk to her, and that she would get back to me. At the end of the day, she didn't want Maddy to move away from her. After talking to her until I felt that I was blue in the face, I figured there was only one thing to do. I called a lawyer in my hometown in Michigan, where Lisa was living with the kids. I was not trying to cause trouble between us; instead, I looked at it as keeping my promise to my daughter.

I paid the lawyer's fees, after explaining my situation with her on the phone. She agreed to take up the case. I figured it was going to be cut and dry and easy. She had warned me that it would not, due to the changes of the custody laws over the past few years. Michigan law was that the child no longer could make the decision at a certain age of which parent they wished to live with—that it had to be decided by the court. My lawyer did ask me if I still wanted to pursue this, and I said absolutely. I owed it to my daughter.

After two court hearings back in my hometown, I had lost, and Madyson was to remain in Michigan with her mother. The judge's decision was based on not wanting to separate the children. The sad part was, neither I nor my daughter was afforded a chance to speak at the hearings. The ex-wife's lawyer made it seem as if I was trying to be deviant about gaining custody of my daughter. That was not the case at all. I was simply attempting to grant her wish of living with us, hanging out, and going to school with her friends where we were at. Anyway, my wife and I felt defeated without fair cause.

One morning, I woke up, went out to the kitchen, made a pot of coffee, turned on the news, and logged into my laptop. I got on Facebook and had a friend request. It was Bridget! I didn't recognize the last name, but as soon as I opened up her profile, I immediately recognized her.

"Oh my God!" I hollered out.

I accepted her friend request. Just like I did with Erin when we first became friends on Facebook, I wanted to wait a couple of days before I asked her about Crystal's full name and how to get a hold of her. I didn't want to come off as if that was the only reason I wanted to reconnect with her, but it definitely was up there. I said hello to her and told her how nice it was to connect with her again after all the years that had gone by. I was hoping that she would bring up Crystal to me first, but instead, I just got an "It's nice to hear from you after all of these years. What have you been up to? It's nice to finally link back up with you after all this time."

Like I said, I was going to wait it out for at least forty-eight hours before asking about a possible son in North Carolina, but I couldn't. Instead, the next morning after we became friends on Facebook, I messaged her and asked her if she still had contact with Crystal. She didn't get back to me right away. It was around noon that day when she had gotten back with me. I was so excited when I saw the message icon with a red number one next to it. I knew it was going to be her with an answer for me. The conversation went something like this:

"Hi Bridget, do you remember that girl that I dated in '95 named Crystal? Would you be able to give me her last name please? I would like to contact her, in order to find out about a possible son I may have in North Carolina. It's been dwelling on my mind all of these years. The main problem is that I do not remember her last name, so I don't know how to get a hold of her."

"I'm sorry, Nate," she wrote back, "but I haven't had anything to do with her since you guys were together. I found out what she did to you, and that was it for me. I haven't talked to her since."

I had never looked at it as her doing something to me, but that maybe she had kept something from me. Either way, I just needed to get a hold of her.

"Can you give me her last name please?"

She told me the same thing as everybody else: that she didn't remember what it was. I remember thinking, "Wow! There must be something in the water down there that is giving us all amnesia." Nobody could remember anybody's last name. She did tell me that she thought that her last name was Evans. She said for me to try to find a Crystal Evans from Durham. I thanked her and told her how appreciative I was for anything that she could do to help me with this situation.

"Do me the favor and let me know if you happen to find out anything," I said. "I am very interested in finding out whether I have a son or not."

She assured me that she would.

I searched Crystal Evans, but nothing ever came up except for a couple names, and they didn't look anything like her. I Googled the name, and it was generally the same result—nothing. "Crystal Evans from Durham, North Carolina" was what I kept plugging into the Facebook search. Same result.

At this point, I felt as if it was all over. Bridget was always going to be my last hope, and when she finally found me on social media, it fell through. That was it. There was nobody else who could reconnect us. Erin and Bridget were it, and when they both fell through, I lost all hope of finding him.

On a positive note, the summer of 2017 turned out well for my family. My daughter was finally able to move in with us. It was right before her senior year of high school. Her mother was moving in with her fiancé in a different city, and it was a different school district as well. My daughter had told her that if she was going to move, that she was going to move in with me and Jess in Ohio. Her mom was a little reluctant but gave into her wishes and allowed her to pack up her stuff and move down to Ohio with us. We were all so excited. My son was a little sad, because for the first time in their lives, they were going to be separated. But it was his choice to stay with his mother, and I respected it.

I was still getting him every other weekend. Everything was going great, but I felt that there was something that they needed to know. It would be the first time that Maddy and Taylor were going to hear this. Jessica already knew, because I had talked to her about it several times over the past several years. I had even mentioned it to our friends, the fact that I believed I may have a son in North Carolina.

I figured they were old enough and mature enough to hear what I had to tell them about the situation. They were both sitting in the living room when I broke it down to them. I told them about Crystal and the short time that we were together when I was a young soldier at Fort Bragg.

"I think you two have an older brother somewhere in North Carolina."

My daughter immediately got on her laptop and began looking up a Crystal Evans in North Carolina. I told her that she was probably wasting her time, that I had already been searching over and over again with zero results.

"Well, Dad, at least I can try my methods of searching."

At this point, Maddy had been already searching her family trees on both sides of the family. On my side and her mom's as well. She had discovered dates and places of our family history that I never knew about. She was into ancestry research. Her grandmother and grandfather were into it also and had gotten her into it too. She had an interest in it for at least a couple years prior to her moving in with me and Jess. She never did find out anything about North Carolina.

The years went by. Madyson graduated from high school in 2018. She began attending Bowling Green State University, right up the road from our little town. We were very proud of her, especially my wife, since she is an alumni from there as well. COVID-19 had come and gone (well not "gone," but the pandemic was over). My son had graduated the year of COVID in 2020. His class, like every other class of 2020 across the nation, never got a graduation ceremony. The best they could do was take some pictures in their caps and gowns. Their class made the best of the circumstances.

Three years went by, and it was winter of 2023. My daughter had graduated from BGSU and moved back up to Michigan. She had an apartment and a job at a cancer treatment clinic, after majoring in health and human services. At the same time, she was studying for her master's in epidemiology, the study of disease. While she was going to BGSU for her undergraduate degree, she was working at a local town's emergency room, right during the height of COVID. She immediately got interested in disease study.

My son Taylor went right into the workforce when he got out of high school. He has an excellent job working at a Scotts Fertilizer plant in a major farming community in Michigan, where he is highly respected and continues to get raises and promotion offers. I'm very proud of them both. They both have their own places to live. My son and his girlfriend live together in a nice apartment, and my daughter and her boyfriend recently bought a house together. I am very proud of them. They have successfully transitioned from childhood to being self-sufficient in their adulthood. A parent couldn't ask or wish for more accomplishments from their children.

It was two days after Christmas of 2023. I was sitting in the living room watching TV. My phone rang, and it was my daughter.

"Hello, Maddy! How's it going? What's up with you guys?" I asked excitedly.

"Well, Dad, I have some news for you that I think you should be sitting down for."

I immediately thought that she was going to tell me that she was pregnant.

"Oh, yeah. Hey, Dad, is Jessica sitting there with you by any chance?"

"No, she's at work," I said. "Why? What's going on?"

"Okay, that might be a good thing," she replied. By this time, I was becoming concerned.

"Dad, I have been in contact with somebody since this morning, and it's time that you find out."

"Okay, Maddy, spit it out."

"Dad, your beliefs of having a son in North Carolina are true, and I have been in contact with him today. He actually contacted me first and told me that I was his half-sister. Everything that you've been telling me and Taylor is true, and he found me, and contacted me through 23 & Me."

Until I had this conversation with my daughter, I had never heard of 23andMe before. I had to ask her what it was and how it was used. She broke it all down to me, that it was a website used to find family or relatives through DNA results, and that you can message one another through it as well. That was how he had contacted her. His results showed that he had a half-sister, and once he confirmed it, he contacted Maddy.

So, I was taking all of this in as calmly as I could without going into a state of shock. All kinds of emotions were rushing through me when she was telling me all of this. I was excited, I was curious to find out more, I was anxious, I was relieved, you name it. I couldn't wait to tell Jessica when she got home from work.

"Maddy, what is his name?"

"His name is Trey, Dad. He's almost twenty-seven years old."

I got quiet as I thought about his pictures that were sent to me when he was a toddler. I never knew what happened to that envelope. I can only assume that the ex-wife had thrown it out when all of this was coming to light in North Carolina twenty-four years ago. I can vaguely remember that the name Trey was written on the note that came with the pictures.

I didn't say too much as I was taking all of this in. She told me that he and his girlfriend did the 23andMe test, and then once they found out about her being his half-sister, he confronted his mom with it. She confirmed it. She didn't even try to sugarcoat it, but instead, she was completely truthful with him. She had told him that she and his dad had broken up for a little while back in the mid-'90s, and that she had started dating a soldier from Fort Bragg. She confirmed that I was his father. I felt bad when Maddy was telling me this, because I could only imagine what he must have been going through. He found out that the man he thought was his father all his life turned out not to be his biological father. Now, Trey and I believe that he is his father—he is the man who raised him and took care of him from infancy. I remember, when Maddy was telling me about all of this, how I felt that the entire family must be going through some hardship over this. There needed to be a healing timeline for that whole family. Maddy also told me that Trey and his girlfriend had two toddlers. A boy and a girl. I was a grandfather! Talk about a shockwave hitting me that day!

I got off the phone with her and sat in silence. Then I got off the couch, walked to the kitchen, and opened up a beer. I found it to be such a relief, and I was now going to have a few beers and celebrate the confirmation of what I had known for almost thirty years of my adult life. I told myself that I was going to give it some time before attempting to contact him, because I knew that his family needed to digest all of it.

What was killing me during this initial discovery was wanting desperately to see a picture of him. I had asked Maddy if she had seen a picture of him, and she said that she did. She said that she had found him on Facebook. She had confirmed to me that he looked just like us—me, Maddy, and Taylor. Same complexion, hair color, facial structure, etc. She gave me the Facebook link to his page. I went straight to it. Wow! I knew right away that he was my son for sure.

I did wait a few days and then I sent him a friend request on Facebook. He immediately accepted. The next thing I knew, his girlfriend had sent me a friend request. They both requested my wife as well. I had noticed that they were already friends with Maddy and Taylor. He and I began messaging each other, and we went back and forth for a couple of days. Eventually, we exchanged phone numbers and began texting each other throughout the day. He has a great job working for an electrical company. The only problem is that he has to travel all the time, a couple of weeks at a time. His company has a lot of jobs around the southern states. As I am writing this now, he is currently in Savannah, Georgia for the next couple of weeks. He says he hates being away from his family in Newport, North Carolina, but he also says the money is good. His family had moved from Durham to Newport when he was younger, and they live there to this day.

One Saturday evening, I texted him and told him to finally call me when he had a chance away from work. I believe he was on a job in Texas. He called me, and we must have talked for over an hour that first time. He sounded just like I expected he would. He has somewhat of a high-pitched voice, with a strong southern accent. He has an excellent, strong, and positive attitude about life in general. He is a confident person, and a responsible man for himself and his family. I also found out that he is an excellent guitar player. He is in a rock band back home in North Carolina, called Blotter. They are excellent too. The wife and I have listened to a lot of their songs. They also have an album cut, if not two. They have their own YouTube channel, where you can see them perform. They also have their own podcast show.

We talked for quite some time. I felt obligated to tell him the truth of how he came to be. I at least wanted him to hear my version, because I didn't know what he could have been told or not told. After I explained what I could remember from back in 1995 and 1996, he told me that that was what he was told as well. When we got off of the phone that first time, I felt like a thousand pounds was lifted from my shoulders. I'm sure he felt the same way. We were both at ease with our overall conversation. We went back and forth like we were long-lost friends, or even friends at a reunion who hadn't talked to each other in years.

My wife was working night shifts at the time I had talked to Trey that first evening. When she got home, I told her all about him and our conversation. I was talking a hundred miles per hour. I was so excited, and she was too. I have to admit, ever since my daughter told me that he found and connected with her, I have been on cloud nine over all of this. A couple of days later, I called him again, and we talked for a while. I did ask him a question that I was curious about, and I might have already known the answer from talking to that woman who told me about him years ago. I asked him if his dad knew about all of this prior to him confronting them around Christmas. He said that he did know all of these years. I have a lot of respect for that man. I don't know of too many men out there who would accept him and raise him as his own son, knowing what he knew. Earlier, I had mentioned meeting him once or twice while I was dating Crystal, and he was very nice with me. Hell, I remember even having a beer or two with him. After talking with Trey a few times, I realized that they were a tight family all around. One could see that from all of his pictures on his Facebook page. He has pictures from the time he was little up to recent days of his own family.

He sent me many pictures of his two children, and they are adorable. A little boy named Jackson, and a little girl named Isabelle. I have also talked to his girlfriend on speakerphone. She is very nice and has been in constant contact with my wife, which is awesome. My parents, my son and daughter, my coworkers, and my friends are all happy and excited for me and Jessica.

We keep in regular contact with one another these days. My wife and I have sent them birthday presents, and this summer, they are planning on driving up here to Ohio to stay with us. It will be the first time that we will all meet in person. I cannot wait. We are very excited about them coming up here and staying with us. The future is so bright for us all. We are adults who refer to each other as Nate and Trey. We know we are father and son, but we will start off with being great friends, and we are looking forward to having a relationship and a strong bond of friendship with one another.

I am excited to see him for the first time, to shake his hand and give him a hug. I am excited for that vacation time with them this summer. I am excited to hold and hug my first grandson and granddaughter. I am excited that the mystery and wondering about the unknown is finally over after twenty-seven years. I am excited that my son found me.

Myself and my son Trey. Christmas 2024.

My son Taylor, Trey, and myself with my two grandchildren.
A family meeting each other in person for the first time.

ACKNOWLEDGMENTS

I would first and foremost like to thank the corporation of 23andMe. Had it not been for this company, I may have never found my family from North Carolina. I would also like to thank my daughter Maddy and son Trey for applying for 23andMe. Had it not been for the two of them applying, our relationships would probably never have existed. Finally, I would like to thank my entire family, on both sides, for accepting all of this, especially when it happened so suddenly. Thank you all.

www.ingramcontent.com/pod-product-compliance
Lightning Source LLC
LaVergne TN
LVHW041626070526
838199LV00052B/3251